Interdependent Wealth

*How **Family Systems Theory** Illuminates Successful Intergenerational **Wealth Transitions***

STEVE LEGLER

Interdependent Wealth

Interdependent Wealth

Copyright © 2019 Steve Legler
All rights reserved.
ISBN: 9781097309092

© 2019 Steve Legler
All rights reserved. No part of this publication may be reproduced or transmitted in any form or by any means, electronic or mechanical, including photocopying, recording or any information storage and retrieval system, without permission in writing from the publisher.
Canadian Copyright Registration # 1156996
Published by TSI Heritage
Montreal, Quebec

http://ShiftYourFamilyBusiness.com/

Although the author has made every effort to ensure the accuracy and completeness of the information contained in this book, neither the author nor the publisher assumes any responsibility for errors, inaccuracies, omissions or inconsistencies herein. Any slights of people or organizations are unintentional. Readers should use their own judgement and/or consult a financial and legal expert for specific applications to their individual situations.
Editor: Donna Dawson, CPE
Cover design and page composition: by Nancy Morris and Tarek Riman
ISBN: 9781097309092

Interdependent Wealth

ENDORSEMENTS

Thank you, Steve for continuing the effort to understand and explore just what is meant by "thinking systems".

Most people will say that a family is a system but not everyone has a notion of just how it is "a system" and how that perspective relates to the life transactions that impact our businesses and wealth transfer.

Thank you for taking all of us just a bit further on that road to understanding and action.

Kathy Wiseman
- Co-founder of Navigating Systems DC, an educational forum for family enterprises and families of wealth.
- Faculty Member of the Bowen Center for the Study of the Family at Georgetown
- Co-author of Trustworthy, New Angles on Trusts from Beneficiaries and Trustees.

*Steve Legler combines insight, knowledge, humor, and candor in a book that
will enable you to take a fresh look at your family business.
Amazon lists 40,000 books under "Family Business,"
and I'd bet money that this is
one of the most original, and most useful.*

Mitzi Perdue
Speaker and author of How to Make Your Family Business Last

*Understanding family systems theory and action are essential
for understanding family businesses.
Yet there are few resources specifically discussing Bowen Family
Systems for families and advisors working in this field.
Steve Legler has thankfully provided us with a readable, down-to-earth, and straightforward introduction to how affluent
business families operate from a Bowenian perspective.
It is a long-overdue addition to the family enterprise literature.*

James Grubman PhD
Global family wealth consultant and author of Strangers in Paradise: How Families Adapt to Change Across Generations.

*Pragmatic, Prudent and Precise. Steve gives readers all three Ps
to understanding Bowen's Family Systems Theory and applying
it to their unique circumstance. This book deserves a front row
spot in your professional library!*

Kirby Rosplock, PhD
Speaker, consultant and author of The Complete Family Office Handbook and The Complete Direct Investing Handbook

Interdependent Wealth

Interdependent Wealth

CONTENTS

Introduction. Laying the Foundation ... 1

Part I. Subject Matter Context ... 9

Part II: Useful Overlaps ... 27

Chapter 1. Me and/or We ... 29

Chapter 2. Art and Science ... 37

Chapter 3. Mapping It Out ... 45

Chapter 4. Anxiety ... 57

Chapter 5. Rewards for Conformity ... 67

Chapter 6. Put Me In, Coach ... 77

Chapter 7. How Can't I Help You? ... 85

Chapter 8. Informal Connections ... 95

Chapter 9. Leadership ... 105

Chapter 10. Peer Learning ... 113

Chapter 11. Perpetuation ... 123

Chapter 12. Subjectivity ... 133

Chapter 13. Top-Heavy Triangles ... 143

Chapter 14. The Importance of Unstructured Play Time ... 153

Chapter 15. Simple versus Easy ... 163

Part III. Takeaways and Next Steps ... 171

Appendix ... 175

Acknowledgements ... 179

INTRODUCTION. LAYING THE FOUNDATION

Before getting into the subject matter of this book, I think it's important to properly set the stage. I know that before I spend my time getting into a book by a supposed expert, I like to get a good handle on who the person is and why they think their writing should be interesting and useful to others.

I expect nothing less from others, so it is only natural that I properly set up the context of what you are about to read.

My Calling to the Family Business Space

In 2013, I enrolled in a program in Toronto called Family Enterprise Advisor (FEA). It was a relatively new program that came out of the University of British Columbia's Sauder School of Business, and it was getting such great results that Sauder virtually had no choice but to offer it in Toronto as well. I signed up without much prompting as I had recently started to get bored with simply managing the assets of our small single-family office, which had been created a couple of decades earlier after a liquidity event.

I initially had visions of serving other families like my own on the investment management side of things, but the FEA program lit a different fire under me.

The majority of my classmates came from large organizations that serve business families, and they had been sent to the course to learn the language of family enterprise and find out what makes family businesses tick.

Unlike most of the bankers, accountants, investment managers and life insurance specialists who attended, I had not been sent by my employer to get better at serving an existing family business client base. I wasn't really sure why I was there, but I was looking for something, even if I didn't know what that was.

The next year or so was a heck of an interesting ride. We learned a lot, and I walked away with a new calling. I didn't have much in common with the bankers and accountants and insurance people, but thankfully there were others in the room too, usually standing at the front.

The instructors we had for the FEA program were experienced people who had been working with business families on all sorts of interesting things, mostly on the family end of things and often with little to do with the actual business.

The more I watched and listened, the more I realized that that was what I had come for. But I had never realized this kind of work was "a thing." And even though I had been on this earth for almost five decades, I had yet to discover "my thing."

Until now.

So I had a new calling – or, actually, finally had a calling. And as anyone with a new calling knows, the first thing you do is write a book about your new area of expertise.

Wait, what?

Okay, I guess most people don't go about things that way.

The calling part came in the spring of 2013, and the idea to write a book came in the summer, just before my 49th birthday. My wife, Julie, had been pushing me to write a book for decades, but I had never had enough drive for any subject to compel me to do the work.

I committed then and there to having my first book out in time for my 50th birthday, because I figured if I didn't have a hard deadline, it wasn't likely to happen. I'm happy to say that SHIFT Your Family Business came out in July 2014, with a few weeks to spare.

Family Business or Business Family?

The subtitle of that book was Stop Working IN Your Family Business, Start Working ON Your Business Family. There are two major differences, and that was what I was getting at:

- A family business is a business that happens to be run by a family, while a business family is a family that happens to own and/or run a business.

And

- Too many people get stuck spending too much time working in their business and would do well to spend more time working on their business instead.

I knew too many stories of families where those shifts, from the business to the family, and from working in to working on, just never occurred, and it was usually to the detriment of the entire family. So I wrote that book as a clear message for those families, just as I was entering the field of serving other families.

Blogs Coming out the Wazoo

The book gave me an outlet for my thinking. I had also recently started blogging about family business and family wealth, and I quickly discovered there was no shortage of topics to write about.

The ShiftYourFamilyBusiness.com website has become the place where I make all my content available to readers. I recently surpassed 300 blog posts, and I continue to produce one every week.

But I always knew there would be at least one more book.

Family Systems Theory – Huh?

In the introductory module of the FEA program on family dynamics, one of the learning points was that the family is a system. That seemed like it made sense, but I guess I expected it to become a bit clearer as we moved through the modules over the next few months.

We did cover lots of new ground during the rest of the program, but we never really got back to the family system stuff. I recall reviewing my notes to prepare for the written and oral exams, and I was hoping there wouldn't be too many questions about that.

Bowen Family Systems Theory

I passed the course and got the FEA designation without really getting comfortable with the whole family system thing. But afterwards, I ran across a couple of references to Bowen Family Systems Theory, and I wondered if that's what the FEA course was referring to.

As I Googled the subject, I kept seeing that this BFST was a really good thing to understand, especially for people who work with family businesses. So if it's good for people who work with business families to know this stuff, and I am starting to work with business families and I want to do a great job, I wanted to at least read a book about it.

I began to search for a book that would explain BFST and help me understand what I should know to better work with families who are in business together. I'm not saying there aren't any books already out there that cover this subject, because there are. Sort of.

What I am saying is that the book I was hoping to find, at the time I got interested in BFST from a family business perspective, did not appear in any of my searches. So instead, I decided to sign up for some BFST training, first in Vermont and then in Washington, DC.

The things I learned are fascinating and very useful to me in my work, and I will continue to work to learn more. But I kept thinking back to that book I was searching for, and somewhere along the line I decided that if it didn't exist, maybe I had to write it myself.

And here we are.

Why This Book, Why Me, Why Now

Since beginning my own Bowen journey, I have shared some stories about the learning process with friends, family, acquaintances and colleagues. I have come to many realizations, which I will be sharing with readers over the following chapters.

One of the challenges I'm constantly facing is making complex subject matter simple enough to understand. It isn't always easy for explanations to remain simple, yet still be useful and correct. But I consider simplifying complexity one of my specialties.

As for Bowen Theory, I've already learned so much, even though I am still what most would consider at best a Bowen "intermediate," or maybe even still a novice.

I know more people would love to learn some of the basics, but currently this material is just not accessible enough. I hope that people will read this book and want to learn more and will then find a BFST training program. Others may say, "Cool; I learned something, but this is enough for me for now."

The question of "why me" is partly answered by default: because nobody else has written it yet.

The "why now" comes down to the fact that it's been almost five years since my first book came out, along with the fact that I was due for a break from taking courses and training programs during those five years.

I need to consolidate what I've been accumulating in my brain these past few years and take stock and write about what I've learned. My main audience, as many Bowen colleagues have suggested, is me. "Write it for yourself," they said.

They say the best way to learn something is to teach it to someone else. In many ways teaching is a better forum for this material, because with a teacher-student relationship, there is give and take, so you can quickly adjust when you notice that you are not coming across the way you hoped. Writing a book is less forgiving, so the challenge is bigger, but I'm up for it.

The other reason that now is the time for this book is that while I am by no means a BFST expert, I am at a point where I have learned quite a bit, yet I still remember what it's like to be brand new at this. I remember what it was like to read Murray Bowen's words and shake my head and wonder, and then think I understood, and then realize I still didn't get it. I remember what it was like to say "wow" after hearing faculty members explain things. I'll try to share those important stories when they are useful to understanding the material.

I come from a business family and married into another business family, and I've learned about serving business families and had my calling here. I immersed myself in courses and training programs in coaching, mediation and facilitation, and then leapt into the deep end of Bowen Family Systems Theory training in 2014 for four years. I am not afraid to offer my opinion.

This is not a book by a BFST expert, and it is not a "how to" book by any stretch of the imagination. If people read it and feel like they learned something useful, I will consider it a job well done.

Interdependent Wealth

PART I. SUBJECT MATTER CONTEXT

A. WEALTH

My View on Family Business and Family Wealth

The title of this book is *Interdependent Wealth*. In many ways the book examines the intersection of two areas of study in which I have great interest: family wealth, and family systems theory. The title represents the two major aspects of the subject I am covering.

I've already touched on the fact that colleagues in the intergenerational wealth transition space may be interested in family systems theory. There are also people who come from the field of family systems theory who are interested in the family wealth space. So this part of the book provides a baseline and a context on which the rest of the book stands.

The vast majority of family financial wealth comes from family businesses, where one or more family members work hard, work smart, persevere, get lucky, make good decisions, take advantage of opportunities, avoid big mistakes, take calculated risks and end up making a lot of money.

Sometimes they were just trying to provide for their families and survive, and things went well and they kept on going.

Sometimes they crashed and burned once or twice before finding the magic combination and having sustained success.

Sometimes they ended up being sole owners after buying out partners who were unwilling or unable to contribute their share during the tough early years.

Sometimes they needed to scrounge up "love money" from family and friends, and sometimes they paid it back and everyone was happy. Other times some family members felt left out and family relationships never recovered.

There are also executives who work for companies that become moonshots, and those people end up making a relative fortune and then decide they'd like to share their financial wealth with their families. There are also professionals who make a lot of money at their job who end up with more money than they know what to do with and have a desire to share it with their family.

These variations all have a few main points in common:

- A considerable amount of financial wealth
- A family with whom to share that wealth
- A decision to share the wealth with the family
- A realization that this financial wealth needs to be looked after

Hopefully, somewhere along the way, there is also a realization that wealth is more than just money.

Give a Man a FISH: The Other Kinds of Capital

In the past couple of decades, many authors have written about the fact that wealth is composed of much more than just money.

Yes, financial wealth is top of mind, the thing that most people think of when the subject of wealth is broached, and something that everyone can quickly grasp – it's the number that comes after the dollar sign, and the number of zeroes that follow it. While financial wealth is important, and while most of the other kinds of wealth we will discuss aren't brought to the surface in the family context when there's not a lot of financial wealth, it must be remembered that financial wealth alone is rarely enough for a satisfactory life.

FISH stands for financial, intellectual, social and human. Some authors add another S, for spiritual. These are the other types of capital.

The most important thing about these other capitals is that they are intangible; that is, they are hard to see and quantify. But they are definitely there, if we take the time and make the effort to look for them and understand them.

The other important point to recall is that while financial wealth is the easiest to see and talk about, families that only care about, talk about and deal with financial wealth are missing the boat and putting the family wealth at risk.

James E. (Jay) Hughes, in his books on the subject, talks about how financial capital must support the other capitals, but not be the sole focus. Briefly, these other capitals are defined as follows:

- **Intellectual:** Our brains, education, training, talents
- **Social:** Our networks, friendships, access to people, community
- **Human:** Our hearts, values, connections, passions
- **Spiritual:** Whether religious or not, a belief in a higher power and a bigger reason for wanting to do good, and a powerful force that keeps a family together

Family Wealth Challenges

Wealthy families, despite their financial resources, do have their share of challenges. The fact that they are well-resourced and can hire the best professionals poses an additional challenge.

Let's just say that when you have a lot of money, you may have a lot of friends, and some of them are not really the right kind of friends.

Depending on the size of the community in which the family lives, and how well known the family is within that community, there is the added challenge of the fishbowl affect. And of course there is little sympathy for the "poor little rich kids" and their problems.

Many people see only the financial wealth, and that includes many of the professionals that a family relies on. Family businesses and families of wealth have all sorts of accountants and tax experts, bankers, lawyers, trust specialists and insurance providers who advise them on the structural aspects of housing the financial wealth to ensure preservation and growth. There is never a shortage of smart people with great ideas that can technically put the family's financial wealth into a more favourable state.

Often when a family has completed a months-long exercise of planning, organizing, restructuring and signing a bunch of documents relating to estate and legacy planning, they let out a huge sigh of relief and think they are done with this subject for a long time, hopefully forever.

What many families leaders neglect to do, at their peril, is to actually involve the people in their families who are stakeholders in those plans and structures.

The field of purposeful planning is a relatively new one, but it is growing. The Purposeful Planning Institute is at the forefront of this field, and the people it brings together as thought leaders and collaborators are second to none.

My definition of purposeful planning includes a few important aspects:

- It is high-level, strategic planning. It is much more than a couple of tactics to save taxes or shield assets.
- It involves collaboration among various skilled professionals. Nobody can be an expert in all the details.
- The family is at the heart of everything. The family's needs drive all the planning.
- Simplicity trumps complexity. The plan must be easily explainable and the family must understand it.
- Beneficiaries are empowered by the planning. It isn't about how to restrict what following generations can do, it's about empowering them.

I recognize that looking at family wealth from the perspective of purposeful planning reveals my own bias. I also recognize that this way of thinking about family wealth is far from mainstream.

I am quite confident, however, that I am on the right side of history and that those who follow this way of thinking about and planning their intergenerational family wealth transitions will be more successful than those who choose not to.

I have been writing about family business, business families, family wealth and enterprising families in my blog at ShiftYourFamilyBusiness.com since 2012, and my biases are pretty consistent. I espouse family communication and making plans for the family, by the family, even though that is not the most efficient or convenient way to go.

There are lots of professional advisors from various specialty fields who have decades of experience assisting families with the technical side of the contents and structures necessary to carry out these sorts of plans, and I have great respect for their abilities. But in isolation, these tactics, while solving some part of the problem, often come with a number of unintended consequences that are actually not good for the family, and sometimes they're even bad for the family in the long run.

Planning for intergenerational wealth transitions is important work that should not be rushed. It is difficult to accomplish properly when the process involves only the wealth creator and a couple of top advisors. "Why would anyone want to get their kids involved in this?" is a question that some may ask. My answer is this: Because you want it to actually work!

B. INTERDEPENDENCE

Learning Bowen Family Systems Theory

In the same way as the last section was a kind of primer on wealth transitions written from my viewpoint, I will now lay out a primer on family systems theory. We need to begin by clarifying some aspects of the field that took me a while to figure out myself, including some that I still do not completely comprehend.

Please recall that this book makes no promises to be the definitive reference on family systems. It is written by one motivated person and it discusses and attempts to explain some of the interesting overlaps of two fields: family wealth transitions and family systems theory, hopefully helping to answer these questions:

- What aspects of family systems theory are useful to those who work in the field of wealth transfer?
- When people say it's good to understand family systems theory when working with family businesses, what do they mean?

As I mentioned earlier, when I first heard of Bowen Family Systems Theory, these were the kinds of questions I had, and I had hoped to find a book to get me started in understanding the answers.

Family Systems Theory

When I first learned that the family is a system, the name "Bowen" did not appear anywhere. Family systems theories exist in different forms, and different people from various fields over the past many decades have espoused their own versions and theories.

I've never studied any theory other than the one put forth by Dr. Murray Bowen. So I will be talking about Bowen Family Systems Theory.

I have heard some of the names of other family systems theorists, but never felt it would be of interest for me to become expert enough in the field to compare the theories. So I will be writing only about my experience and training in BFST. As I've said, I'm not a BFST expert. I have, however, taken great interest and spent a lot of time since 2014 in Bowen training programs. I'm not even sure there was such a thing as a certificate in Bowen Theory when I started down this road, but according to a recent Google search, a couple of programs are trying to formalize the education, and that's probably a good thing.

Bowen Training Programs

In the summer of 2014, as I got interested in BFST, I searched for ways to learn more. After some internet searches, it became apparent that there was one place from which all things Bowen originated: The Bowen Center, in Washington, DC, was where Dr. Murray Bowen himself started the post-graduate program in BFST. A quick look at the Center's website told me that as a newbie in this field, this was not the place for me to begin.

My formal education was in business, with a Bachelor of Commerce degree from McGill University and an MBA from the

University of Western Ontario's Ivey Business School. There was no way this theory from a psychiatrist was going to be comprehensible to me.

I decided to search for something a little bit more my speed. Luckily I found the Vermont Center for Family Studies (VCFS). VCFS was in the process of starting a training program in Burlington, Vermont, which happened to be about a 90-minute drive from my home.

The program was set up and run by a couple of former trainees from the Bowen Center's post-graduate program and was modelled after it, albeit in a scaled-down version. It seemed like the perfect introduction for me. Meetings were one day per month from September to April.

So I signed up and ordered the textbook, *Family Therapy in Clinical Practice* (FTCP), essentially a compilation of all of Murray Bowen's publications and presentations from the 1950s until his death in 1990. We were assigned the first six chapters of FTCP, to be read before the first session in September. I got my copy just in time for our trip to the cottage, so I took it along without even opening it.

Reading Murray Bowen's Words

I will admit up front that I immediately began a love-hate relationship with that book. We got settled at the cottage and one afternoon I decided to start my reading out on the deck. I sat down and opened up Chapter 1, only to see the title "Treatment of Family Groups with a Schizophrenic Member." I went back inside the cottage and told my wife that I was suddenly unsure about what I had signed up for with this Bowen stuff.

But what the heck; I'm here, I've got the book, I know how to read, what's the worst that can happen? Within an hour, I was back inside, waving the book in front of my wife's face, saying, "Wow, this Bowen stuff is *amazing!*"

That said, those first six chapters were a pretty tough slog for someone who had had only one psychology course in his life.

The love-hate part of it has a lot to do with the format of the book. As the initiator of Bowen Theory, Murray Bowen did not sit down one day and write out his theory. He was figuring it out as he went along, and he was publishing and sharing what he was learning every so often at conferences among colleagues, many of whom were quite skeptical about what he was doing and claiming.

The first copyright date on FTCP is 1978, more than 20 years after Bowen started writing about his work. The book is simply a chronological compilation of his writings and presentations over the years. And there's lots of repetition.

The good news is that there's lots of repetition. On many occasions while reading, I had déjà vu, thinking, "Wait, I've already read this." Of course it was true, because parts of text that Bowen wrote as a paper one year naturally restated much of the background that had been written the year before, or even several years before. It seems he was too busy figuring out his theory to sit down and write a nice summary of it in a book.

The good part of the repetition is that Murray Bowen was very good at writing clearly. He chose his words carefully, and even a layman like me could understand pretty much everything he wrote. There was just so much of it, and it was all interconnected in so many ways that it really takes a long time to understand it all.

Course versus Training Program

It was in March of my first year in the VCFS program that I had a bit of an ah-ha moment. I thought that I had signed up for a course on Bowen Theory. The "course" was set to end the following month with our final session.

Imagine my surprise when the instructor asked who among the students was planning on returning next year. I had a confused look on my face as I raised my hand. "I told my wife I was taking a course that ended in April. If I tell her I'm doing it again, she will think I failed the course."

The mysterious world of Bowen Theory was slowly becoming clearer: This was not a course, it was a training program. Recall that I said it was modelled after the program at the Bowen Center. Guess what? That's not a course either. It's not a course because there is no exam, no diploma, no written assignments, no certificate, nada. In fact many people return, year after year, to continue their training. Some go for a few years, take time away, and return.

As I have tried to describe this world to others, the best analogy I have is an exercise or yoga class. There is a regular schedule, and you sign up and show up. There are skilled, experienced leaders at the front to guide you, but in the same room with you there are beginners, intermediates and advanced trainees. Some people will come back over and over; some will stop after a year or even after one session.

The material repeats itself, or maybe it just rhymes, but what you learned on the first pass and what you pick up a year later once you've absorbed the essence will be different.

The Eight Concepts

It is tempting to get into the eight concepts of Bowen Theory so that I can look smart and show you what a good student I was. But I must admit that there are other books that cover the *basics* of BFST much better than I could. And if you are the kind of person who wants to be able to recite the eight concepts and explain what they mean one by one, then this is probably not the right book for you. Of course, just as leaving a periodic table out of a chemistry textbook would be a glaring omission, I would be remiss if I did not at least include the list below.

The Eight Concepts of Bowen Theory[1]

- Triangles
- Differentiation of Self
- Nuclear Family Emotional System
- Family Projection Process
- Multigenerational Transmission
- Emotional Cut-Off
- Sibling Position
- Societal Emotional Process

I can tell you that there were a few basic concepts at the beginning, and Bowen eventually added a few more, including Sibling Position, which he added after being exposed to the work of Walter Toman. His eighth concept, on societal emotional process, was not really ever fully formed, and there was even a reported ninth concept that was leaning towards the supernatural, which had only scant coverage.
My point here is that taking Bowen's work and labelling what important idea is part of which concept is not necessarily a

---

[1]Roberta M. Gilbert. *The Eight Concepts of Bowen Theory*. Leading Systems Press, 2004.

worthwhile endeavour. The important parts of the theory are all interrelated, interconnected and *interdependent*.

Systems Theory Basics

A system is made up of several different components that function together in an interrelated or interdependent way. Here are a few key points:

1. A system is not simply a collection of components. The solar system is not just a list of planets and moons; they are interrelated. Isn't it amazing that whenever there is an event like an eclipse, scientists can tell us that it will happen again in exactly 42 years, 3 months and 11 days? That's because they have figured out how everything is interrelated.
2. The interrelationship of the components is often the most interesting aspect of many systems, especially those whose components are people!
3. In theory, if one component changes, the other components will also change in response.

Remember the first chapter of the Bowen book, which looked at people with schizophrenia in a family? Murray Bowen was working with patients who had schizophrenia, and he theorized that the "problem" that everyone assumed was inside the patient's head actually came from their family relationships. That's where his theory began. He was convinced that the interdependence of the family was the root of the problem. This is not to suggest that schizophrenia is not a real condition. I am not attempting to minimize it, I'm simply noting where Bowen began working on his theory.

Long story short, when dealing with "problem" teenage patients, he eventually often preferred to not even see or treat the "patient," focusing instead on the parents and their relationship with each other, and lo and behold, the "problem child" improved. He knew he was on to something, and he made it his life's mission to prove it.

Bowen's hope was that eventually, this could all be so clearly explained that it would be considered a science, yet he was realistic in his expectation of the timeframe that would require. He knew it would not be in his lifetime and suggested it could take decades or a century or more.

Common Uses of BFST

The fields that seem to have the most activity relating to Bowen Theory are psychology, social work and clergy. During my two years in the post-graduate program at the Bowen Center, I came across lots of people who were therapists or social workers, as well as people from various areas of clergy of every denomination. There were a handful of people who, like me, worked with families on their intergenerational wealth transitions, but we were certainly in the minority.

Learning by Doing

"If this stuff is so great, how come more people aren't talking about it?" I've heard this question since I started down the Bowen road. I am several years in, and I think I'm getting closer to the answer.

Just to recap, I did return for a second year in Vermont, having explained to my wife that I did not fail the course, but that I had chosen to continue the training. As the second year was wrapping up, I started to think about writing this book, because as far as I could tell, the book I was looking for still did not exist. As I toyed with the idea of writing the book, I knew that if this were ever going to happen, I needed to kick it up a notch and go to Mecca. I needed to enroll in the program at the Bowen Center.

I have now completed two years of training in the post-graduate training program there. Did I pass the exam? There was no exam. Did I get a diploma? No, they don't give diplomas. Do I now know everything I need to know? No, but I'm getting there, and I know that I will never get there.

So what if I could recite the eight concepts and explain them clearly to anyone – wouldn't that be enough? Maybe for some people that would be plenty. But once you get inside the Bowen tent, understanding what Murray Bowen was working on is no longer enough. As I like to say, there is no shallow end in the Bowen pool.

And to continue the swimming analogy, imagine that you had read and studied everything there is to know about swimming but had never been in the water. You could be a theoretical swimming expert, but if I took you to the middle of a lake and threw you in the water, well, what then?

The "culture" of those who study BFST has a strong influence and drive towards action. You can't just learn Bowen Theory. Well, you can, but why read a book on swimming if you aren't going to swim?

It gets a bit scary when you realize that if you really want to learn it, you have to do it. I have now done some of the actual swimming part, and it feels good (come on in, the water's fine!).

It isn't for everyone, though.
But that's part of my reason for writing this book. I want people to understand what's involved in learning this stuff, and how it can be so useful, whether it is for your own family or for families you work with.

There is some really eye-opening stuff that comes from doing the work. Bowen seems to have stumbled upon this aspect himself when he noticed that some of his students who worked on their own relationships within their families of origin would report positive changes in their lives and their ability to function better with others.

Bowen then used himself as Exhibit A and experimented with his relationship to his own family of origin to prove his points.

I hope the rest of this book will give you reasons to want to learn more and maybe even take up the challenge yourself. I would love to see BFST become more popular. At the same time, I understand that for most people, it is too much work, and the work itself is not always easy. It does get easier, but it's never really easy.

But think about it: if you want to understand human relationships, you're probably going to have to work out some human relationship stuff where you are one of the key humans being studied. And if you want to understand family relationships, it stands to reason that you are going to have to work on your family relationships too.

Sounds pretty simple. But remember: simple doesn't necessarily mean easy.

Interdependent Wealth

PART II: USEFUL OVERLAPS

We are now getting to the meaty section of the book. I feel like I have laid out enough context, and hopefully enough incentive, for readers to jump into the essence of what this book is supposed to be.

With my work in the family business/family wealth space I have formed certain views on the ways that families can increase their chances of successfully transitioning wealth to successive generations.

I have also been a student of Bowen Family Systems Theory since 2014, working on finding the key areas from BFST that influence family wealth transitions the most. This section of the book attempts to demonstrate and explain some of the most interesting areas I have discovered.

This examination is far from exhaustive. If ever there is a follow-up to this book, it would most likely be a continuation of Part II, giving even more examples of areas from BFST that are useful for family businesses and their advisors to understand.

I will weave BFST concepts in with elements of family wealth transitions and attempt to provide insights into the questions that are useful to families themselves, to their advisors and to individual members of those families. After all, when a family is "stuck" and requires a change to get unstuck, those changes are usually the result of the drive and actions of one motivated family member. It is my hope that this book can serve as a catalyst to such family members and as a resource to their advisors – and ultimately as an impetus for change for the family.

CHAPTER 1. ME AND/OR WE

GOING FROM "MY WEALTH" TO "OUR WEALTH"

There are surely examples of people who achieved great financial wealth but who did not have a family with whom to share it. Perhaps they died and left everything to a charity they held dear.

If only every case were so simple.

Usually people who become financially wealthy do so in the context of a family, even if they are the only person from the family working in the business at the outset. As soon as there is a spouse or significant other involved, things already begin to change. But it is with the arrival of children that everything changes for real.

Once again, there are certainly exceptions – people who made a lot of money and for whatever reason their children were never in the picture as far as sharing in that wealth. We've all heard of people who have made it big and yet are so intent on not spoiling their children that they have made it clear that their kids would get nothing.

I will not judge those people here (or anywhere); as long as they are clear in their intentions and actions, good for them. But for the vast majority of people who end up accumulating significant wealth, as soon as they have a family, they begin to consider their wealth to be "our wealth" instead of "my wealth."

There is something about becoming a parent that makes this natural. Anyone who has had the privilege and pleasure of holding their newborn child in their arms knows the feeling I am talking about. This tiny creature is a part of me, it is counting on me, and I need to provide for it and do everything in my power to protect it. Whatever is mine is ours, and I will sacrifice everything I have for its wellbeing.

But when we fast-forward 30 or 40 years and we still think of that child as a baby who needs protection, this can be a problem.

As parents watch their offspring grow up, they take many different approaches to sharing their wealth. Some lavish gifts and cash on them in order to feel good and keep the kids happy. Others go to the other extreme and hold on to every penny for fear of making life too easy for their kids. Of course, there are many approaches closer to the centre of that continuum that are more moderate, more reasonable and ultimately more conducive to good long-term results.

At this point I am only referring to sharing the wealth itself, as in writing cheques and giving money to the kids. As the children grow older, managing the money gets trickier when you get to the stage of deciding who has input into where the wealth goes.

Again, there is a wide variety of strategies, running the gamut from top-down autocratic decision-making to family meetings where people convene and make decisions through consensus.

I think a lot of people get stuck on these questions about what to do with the money, which is unfortunate. By that I mean it is easy to do things a certain way for certain reasons at a certain point in time, and then get stuck in those ways, even when they are clearly no longer appropriate.

It is easy to think of that infant in your arms on the day they were born and continue to feel like you need to hold them like that.

When you change your baby's diaper, if you fast-forward in your mind to the day when you may be wearing diapers and this child, or someone they have hired, will be changing your diapers, you may look at things differently.

This is my first hint about what the word "interdependence" means to me, and it has to do with the timeframe that we use to look at life.

There will be years and even decades when it will be clear that you are at the top of the pyramid in your family, the one who makes decisions and holds the power. It will not last forever; it never does. You came into the family as a baby and hopefully you will go out as an elder who had a really good run, but in a perfect world you will not go out "on top."

That's enough about my own philosophy for now. I said that I'd weave in some Bowen Family Systems Theory, so here goes.

The Individual–Togetherness Continuum

Murray Bowen talked a lot about the natural forces of togetherness in a family. It is only natural that family members be strongly attracted to being and staying together, because when we go back a few generations (okay, many, many generations) there was a lot of danger in the world and staying together was a matter of survival.

In his work, Bowen talks about how when a man and a woman meet and form a couple, every couple will have its own "level of fusion." Some couples are naturally inclined to think of themselves as a "we" as opposed to "you and I." (Keep in mind that during Bowen's career, from the 1950s to the '80s, just about every example dealt with heterosexual couples who would marry first and then have children. Gender roles in the examples were also pretty "traditional," based on the era.)

The opposite of the togetherness force is the force to become an individual. In everything we do every day, we are constantly choosing between what is best for me and what is best for us. Luckily most of these choices are not either/or questions, and there are plenty of win-win outcomes.

Differentiation of Self

Bowen's cornerstone concept is the differentiation of self scale. It is a theoretical scale that runs from 0 to 100 and indicates where people stand in terms of their ability to think and act for themselves as opposed to simply following the group. When I say it is theoretical, I mean that Bowen threw it out there as an idea, as a way to think about the concept.

A certain portion of BFST training involves watching videotapes of Dr. Bowen explaining the various concepts of BFST. I began studying Bowen more than 20 years after he died, but because he was an early believer in videotaping his lectures, after watching hours of him speaking, I feel like I knew him.

A typical day at the Bowen Center involves watching two or three 30-minute segments, which are always followed by a 30-minute discussion led by a faculty member.

The video quality is actually pretty good, considering the early ones were in black and white, his main tools are a blackboard and chalk, and in many of them he is smoking a cigarette. I've seen a few of the tapes more than once, and I always get something new from them.

On some of the recordings where Bowen is explaining the concept of differentiation of self, he mentions with frustration that others in the field who have heard of his "scale" have written him letters asking for a copy of the scale. His frustration stems from the fact that if they read his work they would understand that the scale is only a concept, and if you can put a zero at the bottom left of a piece of paper and a 100 at the top left, voilà – you have the scale!

The scale of differentiation is at the heart of many Bowen concepts, which is why I wanted to start this section with some discussion of it. The scale also fits nicely with the me/we question around wealth, and whether it belongs to a person or a group.

Let me cover a few of Bowen's basic premises about the scale of differentiation. Bowen theorized that people's differentiation level was more or less fixed by the time they reached adulthood. Once you are an adult, you can try to increase your level, but gains will likely be marginal at best. He also believed that people at similar levels of differentiation would be attracted to each other, not only as friends, but as mates and spouses.

The "I-Position"

One of the key ways that people can attempt to increase their level of differentiation is to work on what Bowen referred to as an "I-Position."

To get outside of "groupthink" you need to be able to think for yourself. Not only do you need to think for yourself, you need to be clear and act for yourself too. "This is what I think," "this is what I believe," "this is what I will do, and this is what I will not do" are examples of statements of I-Positions. Of course it is one thing to make these statements and another to follow through and act on them, but you need to start by becoming clear on these thoughts for yourself.

Considerations for families

Families that are concerned with successfully transitioning their wealth from one generation to the next (and hopefully the next, and the next...) should understand that while some togetherness is good, too much is not necessarily better.
It is also important to take a really long-term view of the wealth and look at an appropriate arc of time. If you care only about what happens during your lifetime, that's pretty selfish. It is also short-sighted in many cases, because there comes a time in many people's lives when someone other than you will be making healthcare decisions, so it is advisable to arrange your life in a way that maximizes the chances of others making the best decisions on your behalf.

Considerations for motivated individuals in the family

If you are the person in the family who recognizes that your family needs to work on these family issues but you feel very alone, first of all, bravo. Now what can you do to get others to understand the need (and possibly even the urgency) of getting moving? There is strength in numbers. Who else in the family understands, like you, that some action is needed? Finish reading the book and then pass it on to them.

Considerations for advisors to families

If you are an advisor to a family that seems to be having some difficulties with the me/we questions, or if you see either too much togetherness in the family or none whatsoever, what can you do?

The first thing I would suggest is meeting with more people from the family, such as the spouse and children. When you get other family members around a table you can better assess how well they function together and figure out where future problems may lie. Once you see where the problems are likely to come from, you can begin to plan for ways to deal with them.

If you are still dealing only with one main decision-maker in the family, you are missing the opportunity to become an advisor to the whole family and your relationship with them will likely end right after your contact's funeral.

CHAPTER 2. ART AND SCIENCE

Because Murray Bowen was a medical doctor, he naturally studied plenty of science. As he began working on his family systems theory, he recognized that for it to be respected by other scientists, he needed to work meticulously on the details.

When you and I interact with our parents, spouses and children, though, it doesn't necessarily feel very scientific. Somehow even envisaging a "science of human behaviour" may seem like a bit of a stretch. The way we deal with each other in our families feels much more like an art than a science, at least on the surface.

Transitioning Wealth – Let's Ask the Experts

When a family leader decides to start working out the details of transitioning the family's wealth from the current generation to the next, they will often begin wherever it seems easiest. They will almost always have discussions with the family's expert advisors, usually including accountants and lawyers.

If I asked you whether these folks are more like scientists or artists, I think most would agree they are typically more like the former.

Not many families are experts in what it takes to properly transition their wealth to the next generation. Most families that have managed to amass significant wealth did so in some endeavour or business that most likely had very little in common with what's involved in successfully preserving the fruits of those labours.

Enter the experts.

We will ignore the fact that most family leaders procrastinate when it comes to generational wealth transition. We will instead jump right to the point where they have finally agreed to take care of this, if only so they can then forget about it!

So the leader of the family has finally decided to get the transition plan taken care of, and the family's trusted advisor is called in. Soon a couple of people are tasked with preparing all the documents and structures required to get it done.

What usually occurs in the following weeks and months is a complete examination of all the assets the family owns in order to quantify everything in detail. The accountants and lawyers then strategize to come up with a plan that best meets their main goal, which is of course to demonstrate how smart they are!

The family is hiring and paying the experts, of course, so the experts should be working to achieve whatever goals the family thinks are most important. But as I mentioned, few families know what those goals are at the outset of this process, so the experts kind of fill in many of the blanks themselves.

Most experts will then devise a plan that results in the greatest possible tax savings. There isn't anything inherently wrong with minimizing the amount of tax the family will owe. My contention is that it should not be the only thing considered, or even the most important thing. But of course when an expert can show a client that they would pay a million dollars in taxes under the current structure, but if they just set things up in this other, better, newer, state-of-the-art way they would save so many hundreds of thousands, then it's a no-brainer, isn't it?

Precisely the Wrong Way to Plan the Transition

The exact dollar figure that an expert can calculate, very scientifically, gives an allure of precision to the exercise that is difficult to argue. When you combine this apparent scientific precision with the fact that the client doesn't necessarily know what they really want, other than to get the whole exercise over with, the transition plan will often simply be executed as presented and filed away.

When wealth transition planning is done this way, it is a huge missed opportunity.

Whatever the result of the structures, agreements and contracts that were put together for that transition plan, you can be sure the people who will have to live with the results of the plan will be in for some surprises. And not all surprises are good surprises; in fact, most are not.

What if, instead of starting with the family's assets and figuring out how to prepare them for the heirs, we started with the heirs themselves?

Preparing the Heirs for the Assets

I'm not sure who gets credit for the expression "preparing the heirs," but I am a big fan of it. Too many families engage advisors to prepare their assets for their heirs, instead of preparing the heirs for the assets.

In cases where there is only a single heir, preparation can be relatively simple. When there is more than one heir, well, now you are looking at family dynamics and the relationships between the heirs.

Structures vs. Relationships, Hard vs. Soft

The beauty of setting up structures is that once they are created, you don't have to think about them anymore. The problem with setting up structures is that once they are set up, nobody thinks about them anymore. They are assumed to be adequate. You don't need me to explain to you what happens when you assume.

Relationships and family dynamics are a bit of a different story. Here, we are looking at things that always seem to be in flux. We are seemingly no longer in the land of science, but very much in the land of art. Plenty of people still refer to the differences I am getting at – the differences between structures and relationships – as "hard" versus "soft." While that is not my preferred terminology, I can go with it when necessary. Although I much prefer "science" versus "art," I'm not sure if there is a scientific method one can undertake to address family dynamics and emotional relationships. But that doesn't mean you should ignore them.

Family at the Centre

Instead of starting with experts who will figure out how to save taxes and preserve assets in iron-clad structures, wouldn't it make more sense to first take the time to figure out what you would like your family relationships to look like from the family's perspective?

Of course if you want to figure out who should end up owning and controlling what assets, that is going to entail having some discussions with family members. There is an art to conducting those kinds of conversations, but if you make those decisions without talking about them first, there's a good chance you'll end up with something precisely crafted to accomplish the wrong thing. There is no point in getting the little details exactly right when you've answered the wrong question.

Back to Bowen: Learning BFST versus Living It

We talked earlier about Murray Bowen wanting his theory to be treated as a science, so he was always getting his students to take careful notes of all their observations to catalogue everything. As someone who spent a few years trying to learn BFST, I can say that I really appreciate how much detailed work went into the science.

But even though Bowen and his followers have been continuously striving to have the theory accepted as science, the practical application of what we learn is much more of an art.

In Part I of the book I used a swimming analogy for learning BFST, and I want to get back to that now.

I'm sure that plenty of scientists have studied swimmers and come up with ways to make people swim faster and more efficiently. When you get right down to it, though, when it comes time to use BFST in your life, it sure doesn't feel very scientific. When you are trying hard to work on increasing your differentiation of self, it's not a matter of remembering a formula from a textbook.

When you are in a room with other family members and a discussion is taking place and you can sense that the level of anxiety is already high, and you are trying to instill some much-needed calm, it kind of feels like you are flying by the seat of your pants.

Science Is Fine, But Art Is Where It's At

Here is how I'd like to conclude this art versus science chapter, looking at the worlds of BFST, interdependence and wealth transitions.

"Yes" to science – the more exact and better informed we are, the better results we can hope for. Science can really help to make things as efficient and understandable as possible. If we want to do things that will actually be worthwhile and workable and effective, however, then we would do well to make sure that we also concentrate on the art of what we are doing. We need to consider exactly what we are trying to do, and for whom, and involve those people at the earliest possible stage.

Considerations for families

There is no reason why you shouldn't have your lawyer and accountant as part of the team of experts who will help you craft the best transition plan for your family.

But please don't start there.

Instead, take the time to consider and discuss exactly what you are hoping to accomplish with your family members first. Figure out the "what," and then engage the experts to figure out "how."

Considerations for motivated individuals in the family

If you are a member of a family faced with questions about whether the family's wealth transition planning has even started, or if it is adequate, or what it looks like, you are in a tricky spot. It is difficult to broach this topic with one's parents without seeming greedy or entitled.

Being gently persistent is my best advice. Engaging whichever parent is most open to the message that you are concerned makes sense, as does enlisting siblings who are also concerned and curious. Being genuinely interested and curious about how the family wealth is currently structured could be a good place to start because it can lead to logical follow-on questions about how things will look in the future.

Considerations for advisors to families

If you advise a family that has wealth to transition, I hope there are some ideas in this chapter that you can buy into, despite the fact that they may make your job a bit more difficult.

Many advisors simply do what their clients ask them to without a lot of questions, because it's easier and much more efficient, and, frankly, who the heck are you to argue with them, when they seem to be sure of what they want?

If you want to do what's truly best for your client, and if you consider that your client is not just one person but the whole family, then I think it's pretty clear that you may want to consider taking things one step at a time. Not only that, you want to take those steps in the correct order.

It shouldn't be too difficult to explain to your client that you are looking out for their long-term best interests, and you want their kids to be your clients too.

CHAPTER 3. MAPPING IT OUT

By its very nature, family wealth is obviously an area that involves a number of people. That includes, of course, the major stakeholders, the family members themselves, for whom all this work is being undertaken. There are the people who own and control the wealth today, and the goal is for the same family to continue to own the wealth well into the future.

But, since we still have not found a reliable route to immortality, we need to deal with the fact that people will die and others will take their places.

Geometric Growth

Some families are really good at growing their wealth exponentially while managing to keep the number of stakeholders small. These families face circumstances that can be relatively simple to deal with.

Imagine the other extreme, where a family has grown a certain limited level of wealth, yet the number of offspring in each successive generation is large. The geometric growth of the family stakeholders can rapidly outpace the growth of the wealth, and this will usually create a completely different set of circumstances and problems.

When lots of people are involved, things get complicated, and it can be difficult to make sure everyone actually understands the true picture of where things stand at any given time.

Once again we are going to look at this topic from both points of view: the interdependent part – that is, the family, and the wealth part – the assets. We'll start with the assets because that will allow me to complete a loop begun in the last chapter.

Providing Some Structure

In the last chapter I used the word "structures" a few times, and I'm going to guess that some readers are less than perfectly clear about what I'm talking about. I don't want to get too deep into the details here, because the picture can get fuzzy quickly and because I will get past my level of comfort pretty quickly too if I try to go too far.

Recall that I was talking about the experts in law, accounting, tax, trusts, banking and insurance, all of whom can be useful in wealth transitions. While the work they do is ultimately for the good of real individual humans, they sometimes use other entities to go about their work.

In the last chapter I relied on the word structure, and here I am introducing the word "entity." Structures and entities can be corporations, holding companies, partnerships, trusts, etc.

When a family gets itself organized to transition its wealth, it will often create one or more of those legal entities to help accomplish those goals.

The family's goals may include minimizing taxes, restricting access to wealth under certain conditions, ensuring that wealth is available to future generations, sharing ownership of assets among certain groups, and making sure that assets end up under the control of certain individuals.

The family's expert advisors know how to assemble the required entities into a useful overall wealth strategy. The more wealth there is, and the more people who are set to become beneficiaries of that wealth, the more complex the strategy will generally get. When the experts are devising the strategy, they usually work with diagrams that visually illustrate who owns what, in what proportion.

That sounds simple enough, and in its most basic form, it is. When there is only "Smithco," owned by the Smith family, and the four kids are going to own 25% each, we can all easily draw a simple representation of that ownership.

By the time the experts get through with their machinations to create trusts and holding companies for everyone, it gets more crowded. Now add the effect of time, where you want to show how things stand today and how that will change after someone dies, triggering all sorts of changes. Now you've got arrows depicting what will happen next, and you can imagine that the structure can become unwieldy.

The internal documents the experts use among themselves will usually end up looking a bit too messy and scary to actually share with their clients. So a simplified, cleaned-up version is often prepared to show the basics without unnecessarily having the client shake their head in bafflement about what has been created.

If we go back to the last chapter, where we looked at science, this more complex diagraming would be the part where we think about formulas we can recall from textbooks that look so complex you are actually amazed that someone has figured out how it all works.

Interdependent Wealth

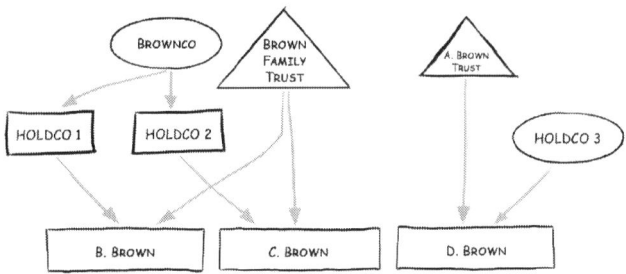

Figure 3.1

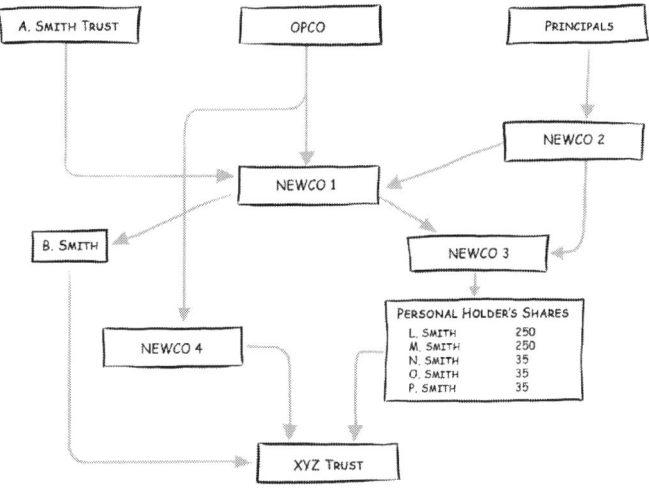

Figure 3.2

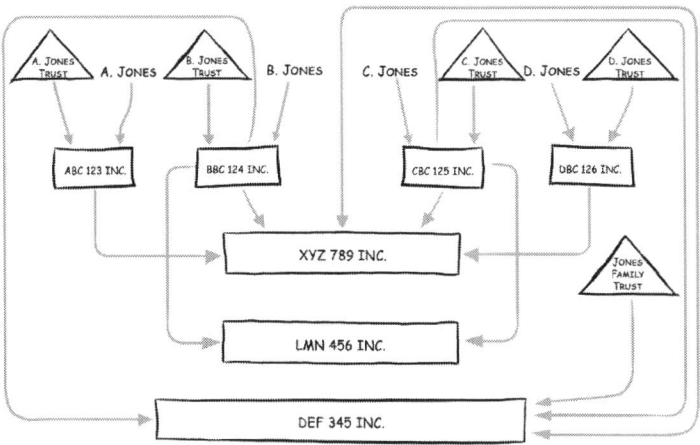

Figure 3.3

The Genogram: A Family Diagram Looking Backwards in Time

Moving over to the "interdependent" side, a whole world of drawing pictures of the way things look awaits. Murray Bowen called these "family diagrams" and in many circles today people refer to them as "genograms." We have all seen various versions of a family tree, and this is essentially what a family diagram is.

A few things in the world of these special pictures are worth understanding and remembering.

When we talked about family wealth ownership a minute ago, we ended with complex diagrams when the experts tried to depict what would happen moving forward in time to a new scenario, post-death, for one of the owners.

The family diagram, for its part, spends most of its time looking backwards in time to one's ancestors.

As I write this on an autumn day on the deck at my cottage, the wind is blowing pretty hard and I can hear the leaves rustling very clearly. So the analogy of a tree is right there for me to grab, and I will. We can all see the tree and its trunk, branches and leaves. But without the roots hidden under the earth, that tree would not exist and could not grow as tall and as wide as it has. The family diagram looks at the roots of the family.

The analogy kind of falls apart if you get hung up on the fact that the roots of the family diagram are usually at the top with the following generations drawn below, but the idea is still pretty good.

Recall that I talked about those black and white videos of Murray Bowen drawing on his chalkboard. Most of what he was doing was drawing pictures of the family examples he was talking about.

A family diagram is a family tree, but it is drawn with some specific conventions, much like the way maps use many common customs for depicting information. For example, as in genetics and genealogy, men are drawn as squares and women as circles. The Bowen people take this pretty seriously – if you ever visit the Bowen Center in Washington, and you need to use the washroom, this information will be useful. I wish I was kidding, but this is how the doors are marked!

As with any other technique or method, the world of the family diagram/genogram has evolved. In addition to the squares and circles, newer conventions have been developed to depict transgender people, with a square within a circle and a circle within a square. Software now exists to help you draw these diagrams by simply entering the relevant information for each person. Interestingly enough, though, many of the Bowen folks I know still prefer to draw these diagrams by hand, including me.

Killing off Your Ancestors

During the post-graduate program at the Bowen Center, part of each afternoon is devoted to small group "supervision" or "consultation" work, where trainees work in small groups with a faculty person as a coach.

Each person takes turns relating a scenario from their life or that of a client or acquaintance, and almost always the person goes to the board and draws a diagram of the family in question. When you draw your own family over and over it's amazing how quickly you can get so many details down in one place. Examples include cut-offs, addictions, diseases, divorce, difficult father-son relationships and any other patterns that seem to "magically" reappear over and over.

As you make progress with this Bowen work on your relationships with your ancestors, you begin to see how important your parents' family of origin was to the way they were, and then how important your grandparents' families of origin were to them. As your coach continues to ask you interesting questions about the facts of your forebears' families, you learn the importance of drawing as many previous generations as you have information for.

An interesting detail is that when a person is dead, their square or circle gets a big X drawn through it. I can recall more than one occasion when I drew a diagram and then remembered that I needed to "kill" the people who were dead. This is done in a very matter-of-fact way, which is part of the whole process, but I can tell you it is easier to put an X through some long-dead ancestor you never knew than it is to put that X through a recently departed family member.

A family diagram that goes back a few generations will invariably lead to some questions and to realizations that history seems to repeat itself.

In addition to the facts that are included, there is also an opportunity to draw in some interpretations as well. There are different ways to symbolize conflict and distance in relationships, as well as certain triangles that show important three-person relationships. We will get into this later, but for now I'd like to share a particular ah-ha moment I had with my own family diagram one day.

My Mother and My Wife

As I share this, please recall that systems thinking tries to get us away from thinking about things in a cause-and-effect fashion. Some things show up on the family diagram that look similar to each other but it's just a fluke.

For instance, after drawing my mother's and my wife's families of origin, more than a couple of similarities became apparent. For example, both are the youngest of five, with one older sister and three older brothers. They have other things in common too.

When you draw the family diagram, you may notice similarities, differences and context that you did not know existed until you drew it.

Interdependent Wealth

A SIMPLE FAMILY DIAGRAM WHERE EVERYONE IS AN ONLY CHILD

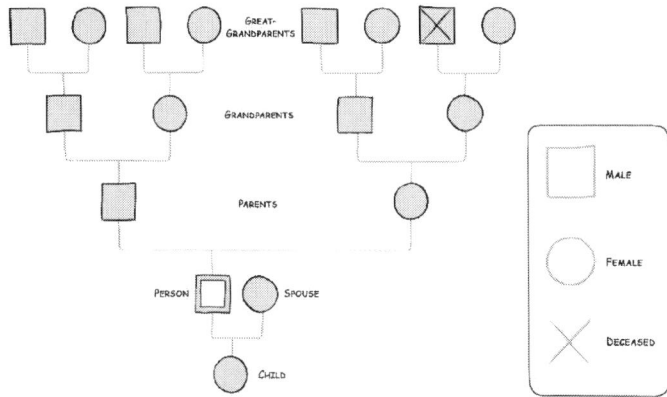

Figure 3.4

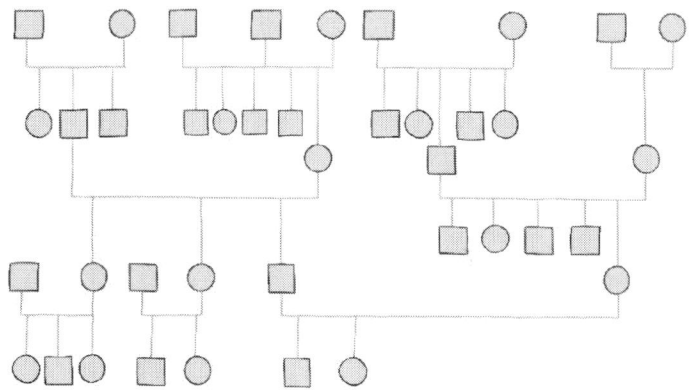

Figure 3.5

This chapter began with a look at how wealth transition specialists typically avail themselves of some complex techniques to attempt to satisfy the many goals of their family clients. The strategies they come up with are often difficult to fully understand without some effort to capture them in a simple visual form so that people can be sure they are all seeing and discussing the plan the same way.

We ended the chapter with a look at how Bowen Family Systems Theory uses a visual representation of the family, which can also be quite complex. But again, without some important ways to simplify a lot of complex information, this stuff would be even more complex than it already is.

Both worlds are full of potential complexities, so it's good to know there are ways to make the information easier to understand. But remember that "easier" to understand is not necessarily "easy" to understand. That said, the more practice you have the better you will get at understanding how these diagrams work.

Considerations for families

When a family decides they need to address the important questions surrounding their wealth transitions, they should know that things can get complicated. Most people already suspect that, and that's usually a big part of why they've put if off for so long. I hope family leaders recognize that they hold the ultimate power in these situations and that they should never get to the point where the outside expert professionals have taken over the process. The family needs to stay in the driver's seat.

If and when the experts present a complex diagram that looks like it's more trouble than it's worth, well, it probably is. Complexity for the sake of complexity, so that your advisors can show you how clever they are, is not necessarily the best way to go. And before you get too enthralled with the diagrams produced by those wealth experts, have you taken the time to map out your family diagram to see what you can learn? You may see patterns in previous generations – related, for example, to family size, health issues, marriage and divorce.

Considerations for motivated individuals in the family

An individual family member who is motivated to take action within their family may come at this "mapping it out" chapter from a few different perspectives. Quite often some estate planning has already taken place, perhaps years ago, and a rising generation member will become curious about "what happens if?" or, more correctly, "what happens when?"

When they gather the courage to ask the questions of their elders, they will typically be told not to worry and that everything is taken care of. "Run along now..." It can be difficult to even ask these important questions, and once rebuffed, you can't just go back again the next day, can you?

Well, you do need to figure out the best person to approach, and the best way and the best time to try again. Sometimes when a group of concerned family members starts to ask questions, you will have more luck in seeing movement.

Considerations for advisors to families

As an advisor to families who are working on the ways they intend to transition their wealth to future generations, I can tell you communication skills are important. If a complex strategy makes sense to you, you need to be able to convey to your client the reasons it makes sense. And being able to work with the other professionals is also something that many advisors would do well to work on doing better.

Lastly, you don't need to understand the whole family diagram going back generations, but you really should work at getting to know the rising generation. If you are concocting structures and drawing up agreements for people you haven't even met, I'm not sure you are doing this right (even if all your competitors are doing it this way too).

CHAPTER 4. ANXIETY

On our journey through the worlds of Bowen Family Systems Theory and intergenerational wealth transitions we've arrived at a particularly juicy topic: anxiety.

Just about anyone who has ever been involved with a family facing the prospect of transitioning their wealth to the next generation will agree that the subject is rarely looked upon with glee and relish. They all know there will be subjects that may not meet with unanimous agreement, and as a result, there is usually plenty of anxiety during the transition process.

We will return to the wealth area later in the chapter, but for now, let's begin with how BFST deals with anxiety.

Anxiety is everywhere in BFST, yet it is not one of the eight concepts. The fact that it was not accorded status as a separate "concept" should not lead anyone to believe it is not important, however. In fact, in Bowen's "textbook," Family Therapy in Clinical Practice (FTCP), the words "anxiety" and "anxious" show up over 500 times! That's a lot of anxiety.

My difficult task here is to highlight the importance of anxiety to family systems theory, leaving you better informed but not more confused than when you started.

A "Systems" View

I think the best way to achieve this balance is to return to the basic premise that we are looking at the family as a system, a group of related people. We are also looking more at the relationships between the people than at what is going on inside the heads of any of the individuals. We are less interested in the corners of the triangles, and more interested in the lines that join them together.

If we accept the premise that a group of related people is a natural system, we can try to understand some of the things that go on within this system by looking at other natural systems.

We are beginning to touch on Murray Bowen's firm belief that humans are more similar to other animal species than different from them. I won't go too far down this road, but you only have to recall a single image from one of those TV shows like Wild Kingdom to get my drift. Picture a meadow full of gazelles or wildebeests enjoying the grass together, when all of a sudden a predator appears. The resulting anxiety is instantly transmitted to every individual animal that is now in danger of becoming the lion's next meal. This happens automatically, without any particular leader making an announcement of the arrival of the threat, or any instructions on what each is supposed to do.

How Does the System Deal with Anxiety?

Of course anxiety is also something that people experience individually. And it is also true that different people experience anxiety differently. But I'm certain that every single person reading this will recall having been part of a group of people who faced an anxious situation together, where the anxiety was "processed" by the group. Anxiety travels through a group of people and gets dealt with in some way.

Lots of emotions are involved in groups of people, and anxiety can accentuate those emotions in many ways. When a group consists largely of family members who have a lot of history together, additional factors will be at work as well, because old family patterns usually come to the fore. Anxiety is a subject that will come up again in future chapters, especially in the sections where we look at BFST. At this preliminary stage, I want to present one major area that Bowen concentrated on, and that goes back to his "cornerstone concept" – differentiation of self.

Differentiation and Anxiety

In its simplest form, Bowen's contention is that the higher one's level of differentiation of self, the better one will be able to handle anxious situations. The corollary is that people with low levels of differentiation will be thrown off by even very minor events that produce anxiety.

This seems to make sense on a gut-feel level for me, but I'm not sure I truly got it when I first learned it. So I think it's worth spending a few more paragraphs on this idea.

Here are some adjectives commonly used to describe people at the higher end of the differentiation scale: mature, level-headed, calm, unflappable, reserved, reliable and predictable.

So when you imagine high-anxiety situations that will affect a group, it isn't hard to understand that the more people in the group who could be described by these adjectives, the fewer adverse effects anxiety will likely have.

On the lower end of the differentiation scale, other adjectives would be used more commonly: immature, reactive, volatile, unpredictable, hot-tempered, aggressive, emotional and high-strung. If a group of people includes even one person described by those adjectives, it is easy to imagine how even a bit of anxiety might adversely affect the emotional field of that group.

Constants versus Variables

Murray Bowen believed that once a person reaches adulthood and leaves the home of their family of origin, their level of differentiation is relatively fixed: your differentiation level was established in the home in which you grew up, and once you leave, it will not change very much.

I can tell you that students of BFST, including trainees at the Bowen Center, are quite often disappointed by that. "If it's already 'fixed'," the thinking goes, "why should I work at trying to increase it"? The answer is that even very small increases, which Bowen believed are possible with much effort, can make a huge difference in one's life.

But the major point I want to make is that if we agree that level of differentiation is mostly constant, then we should probably concentrate more on the other component of this equation, which is much more variable: anxiety.

Wealth Transition Anxiety

Let's get back to the other main subject at hand, intergenerational wealth transitions. We know that families faced with this challenge rarely undertake the necessary important discussions without at least some reticence. Why is this area so fraught with emotion? Let's look at a few of the main reasons.

Death

If people were immortal, we would not have to approach these subjects at all, or at least not with the same underlying assumption – that is, that people all die eventually. The fact that someone's eventual death, even when it is not imminent, is at the centre of the discussion makes it an uncomfortable topic.

Money

When we talk about the subject of wealth, it is very easy for most people's thoughts to go straight to the most easily measured aspect of wealth: financial wealth. Money.

Many families, maybe even most families, never talk about money because it is not for "polite" conversation. Families who happen to have a lot of financial wealth, who you might imagine have more opportunities and reasons to discuss money, sometimes shy away from these conversations even more than "regular" families.

Even families who have a big business with billions of dollars in sales can go from easily discussing huge deals made at work involving huge dollar amounts, to having much difficulty talking about their salaries and bonuses among family members.

Love

If we don't already have enough obstacles with death and money on the table, let's throw in the context of talking about these issues with family members. Let's add love into the mix. Love is easy to talk about among parents and siblings, isn't it? Parents will profess to love all their children equally, and they usually mean it, even though each child is so different from the others. The differences in the children's abilities and needs also colours the conversation.

So fear of discussing family issues can certainly create anxiety, especially when the underlying context of the discussion is how the family is going to do things with money after some beloved family member has died.

Controlling the Variables

So we've established that each person's differentiation level is more or less fixed, and we can't do much to change that. The variable that I am suggesting we work on instead is anxiety. One of the ways we can do that is by setting the right context.

Recall that anxiety moves through a group of people, sometimes instantaneously. The relevant context in this case is the size and composition of the group. When you begin delicate conversations, it is easiest to begin with the smallest group of people first. If you can get a subgroup to understand the situation and some alternatives, you can make some progress and alleviate some of the anxiety at the outset.

As the planning advances, however, I always encourage families to involve the larger group of stakeholders in the process, and not simply inform them of the fait accompli transition plan once everything has been signed, sealed and delivered.

As the group gets larger, it becomes more important to involve the right people in these important discussions. If we go back to the question of systems thinking, it is key to have someone there who sees the system. To ensure that this person does truly see the system, you need to include someone from outside the system.

A Different Last Name

This is where we get to what I like to call having "someone with a different last name" around the table. Remember when you were a kid and you had a guest over for dinner? Everyone usually brought out their best behaviour while the guest was there. This holds true at any age.

In addition to having a different last name, if that person comes from the higher end of the differentiation scale, they will surely also bring some calm to the situation and lessen whatever anxiety is present. When a facilitator brings calm, that calm can be as contagious as the anxiety otherwise might have been.

Considerations for families

If your family is embarking on discussions surrounding wealth transition, you probably already know that some touchy issues could create friction among family members. Hopefully you also recognize that it is better to soldier on and do this work now, knowing that the issues won't simply disappear because you "hope" they will go away. In fact, they will likely get worse with time.

Start slowly, with as small a group of family members as possible. If you can iron out some of the issues and get general agreement, you will create positive momentum for when you expand the group. Try to have as many calm people around as possible to absorb the anxiety, including some from outside the family.

Considerations for motivated individuals in the family

Most of the ideas for the motivated person in the family were covered above, but perhaps identifying potential outsiders to facilitate family discussions could be something to work on.

Please take the time to get to know any advisors you're considering using before you bring them into a family meeting to ensure they will be a good fit. You don't want to realize that you've made a mistake after everyone is sitting around the table.

Considerations for advisors to families

As someone who works with families as an outside advisor, it is crucial for you to understand the role of anxiety and the way it can affect how discussions and negotiations about the transition will go.

My concerns with how things are often done in the wealth transition industry (which you have surely read between the lines already) are mostly about the fact that plans are often made without any thought about how they will actually be implemented.

It's absolutely crucial to making sure that stakeholders who are part of the execution of the wealth transition are all informed in advance about what is going to happen.

If your usual practice is to create a bunch of documents, have them signed by the parents and then file them away until after the funeral, please realize that you are doing a disservice to your clients' families. Keep reading and you will see that it is possible, and much better, to go that extra mile.

Interdependent Wealth

CHAPTER 5. REWARDS FOR CONFORMITY

As we segue from anxiety to conformity, it strikes me that there is a relationship between these two topics. Sometimes anxiety is created when some family members decide they no longer want to conform to family expectations.

So let's talk about conformity now, and I want to begin by using a term that Murray Bowen used in his early days working on the development of his family systems theory.

Undifferentiated Family Ego Mass

Bowen coined the term "undifferentiated family ego mass" and used it for a number of years before abandoning it because it was causing some confusion. But since I don't consider myself a Bowen "purist" and I don't want to be seen as someone flogging Bowen's thinking only in its best form, I want to use that term here because I think it gets at the subject of conformity.

While "undifferentiated family ego mass" doesn't necessarily roll off the tongue, it does convey an image that I think is useful here. When I hear the term, the picture that forms in my head is a tangled mess, or some sort of blob with a number of different items protruding from it. Somehow Bowen's "ego mass" has translated into an "ego mess" in my mind.

So let's run with it.

Recall the individual–togetherness continuum we discussed in Chapter 1, and the fact that often the togetherness forces in a family are naturally much stronger than the individuality forces. The underlying need being expressed there is often related to safety and security, stemming from an earlier time in human history when there was literally strength in numbers and danger around every corner.

The world is not as scary as it was centuries ago, but some parts of our brain make us feel better when we are part of a group. And when the family leaders of a group prefer togetherness, that preference can often be expressed in very strong ways, even as we try to keep them quite subtle.

We're All in This Together

Bowen himself rarely used the term "conformity," but he did use it when describing his scale of differentiation, notably when discussing those at the higher end of the scale (50–75):

"Those in this group have fairly well-defined opinions and beliefs on most essential issues, but pressure for **conformity** is great, and under sufficient stress they can compromise principle and make feeling decisions rather than risk the displeasure of others by standing on their convictions." [2]

I like that quote because it hits on a few key points:

- It mentions how great the pressure to conform is.
- Bowen relates pressure to stress.
- He mentions compromising one's principles.
- He ties in the risk of displeasing others.
- He notes the struggle to stand by one's convictions.

In short, there is a lot in there, and if you have ever been a part of a family that expects you to behave a certain way, and you have different ideas and would prefer to do something else, you know how difficult this struggle can be.

There is sometimes a tendency to acquiesce and stay entangled

---

[2] Murray Bowen. *Family Therapy in Clinical Practice*. Jason Aronson, 1992. Kindle Edition, pp. 163–64.

in the ego mass, which can be followed by feelings of having missed out on something better. People who resist leaving the safety of the family can feel unfulfilled and wonder why they stayed.

As I searched for a clever title for this chapter on conformity, it was the following from Rita Mae Brown that gave me what I was searching for: "I think the reward for conformity is that everyone likes you except yourself."

Stress and Anxiety

I want to make one other connection here on the Bowen angle before moving on to family wealth, and that goes back to the Bowen quote above. He says "under sufficient stress" people can compromise and resist their desire to follow their individual pursuits. But we need to put this quote into the context in which he said it. He was talking about people who are relatively high on the differentiation scale. These highly differentiated people would be affected "under sufficient stress."

But most people do not rank that high on the differentiation scale, and their ability to stand firm is weaker. Higher anxiety has an even greater effect on people who are not as well differentiated, so in fact it often does not take much pressure from the family to keep most people stuck in the tangle of their undifferentiated family ego mass.

The Family Business Calls

Sliding over to the topic of family wealth, I naturally go to the old standby, the family business. As I've said, family wealth very often has its roots in a family business. Although this has begun to change a bit in the past few decades, with many people achieving wealth much more quickly as executives, entertainment and sports figures, and technology titans, in a traditional sense, much of the wealth that exists today in many countries continues to come from family businesses.

While many of the wealthiest families have long ago divested their shares in the operating businesses that created their wealth, plenty of families are still on the same path (they hope!) of creating wealth that will sustain their family for generations to come. I grew up in such a family, as did my wife and many colleagues who have chosen to continue to work in this space. We all have our stories of working in the business part time or during summers, and sometimes for large parts of our careers.

Many people who have worked in their family's business relate similar stories: there are the dutiful sons like me, for whom the path was drawn from birth. This is what is expected of me, I don't want to disappoint the family, I don't have any better ideas, it seems like a pretty good gig, and it certainly is the path of least resistance.

Others arrive in their family business after trying other things, with varying degrees of success and then ending up back in the fold with the rest of the family, for better or for worse.

There are those who start in the family business and are quickly disillusioned, who summon the courage to leave and never look back, feeling as though they have escaped.

Many end up feeling stuck in a place that does not fulfill them, but there does not appear to be any way out. Let's just say that working in one's family business is far from being just another job.

The Three-Circle Model

The world of family business has long been enamoured of the Three-Circle Model, which highlights the fact that every family business involves three distinct but overlapping systems. This being a book about family systems theory, I would be remiss if I skipped the Three-Circle Model. In fact, it was covered in the very first module of my Family Enterprise Advisor program, where I had my calling to this work.

The model consists of the business system, the ownership system, and of course, the family system. The model is depicted with three simple circles, overlapping in a Venn diagram, which results in seven sectors.

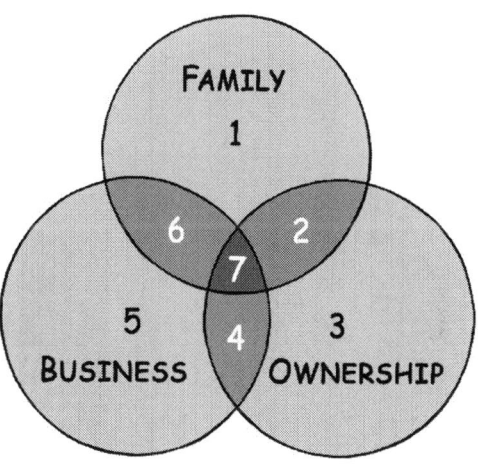

Figure 5.1 The Three Circle Model © Tagiuri and Davis

Getting back to the conformity aspect of the family, everyone who is part of the family is a stakeholder even if they are only part of the family circle. Some families have members who are right in the centre, being family members, owners and employees of the business. Others might be owners who are part of the family but who are not employees. Still others might be employees who are not owners (yet?).

When you consider that a family could have members who inhabit four separate sectors in the model, it's no wonder that family discussions about the business can sometimes be complicated.

There's Good News

When a business family learns about the Three-Circle Model and learns to see themselves through it, they become much less confused – about why people from the same family see things so differently – than before they knew about it. Given the problems with role confusion in family businesses, there really is no excuse for not taking the time to understand these basic ideas.

The first thing that an understanding of the model gives a family is some clarity about everyone's different perspectives. When people can see family and business realities more clearly they can discuss them with others in ways that remove some of the confusion.

Looking at the three separate (yet related) systems – family, business and ownership – allows you to see each of them on their own terms, in their own light and in isolation. What people often end up realizing is that each system has its own membership, its own customs and culture, its own leadership, and its own rules and governance.

Conforming to What?

When we look at the idea of conformity, a question should eventually arise: Conformity to what? Which group are we talking about? Typically, the system with the most pull is the family: there are expectations of conformity to its customs.

If you work in the business, rules of engagement apply to all employees, whether they are family members or not. The conformity aspect is a bit clearer here, although anecdotally, cases of family member employees being treated to a slightly different standard have been reported.

Ownership is a special case, because the ownership of shares in a business is usually something that is carefully spelled out in legal documents. So the conformity questions in this realm are typically relatively clear.

When families move from having a simple operating company further up the wealth continuum towards being a family enterprise, the intersection of the family circle with the ownership circle often takes on more importance than the overlap of family and business.

Together Until

As we wrap up this chapter on conformity, I trust I've left you with some food for thought and an appreciation for the fact that there are some strong forces at play. Relationships will normally stay at some sort of equilibrium for long periods, during which nobody rocks the boat and not much changes.

Of course those periods always come to an end, even if it's only because someone has the foresight to be proactive and plan for the eventual changes that everyone knows are coming.

Considerations for families

If your family is at a point where the status quo is no longer working, you could start by learning the Three-Circle Model and sharing it with other family members. Think about which family members belong in which circle and about each person's permanence in the sector they are now in. Some interesting discussions should be forthcoming.

Considerations for motivated individuals in the family

If you see yourself as an instigator and a "family champion" of sorts, good for you – and good luck. It is easy to get discouraged when others don't believe in the importance of what you are doing.

Keep asking questions and don't worry if your rocking of the boat is bothering some family members. Many of those who are too stuck to act are apathetic because they don't know any other way to be.

Considerations for advisors to families

As someone in whom the family puts its trust, you can use your position as someone outside the systems to help the family leaders see obstacles and opportunities they are not yet appreciating.

I know that many of the family leaders with whom you are dealing are often strong-willed and confident that they know best. If you are someone they trust, and you want to continue to serve them, you need to be able to broach subjects with them that others do not dare bring up.

Interdependent Wealth

CHAPTER 6. PUT ME IN, COACH

Having just completed a chapter about belonging to a family, and perhaps a business system and an ownership system too, we are now going to switch gears a bit and look at how an outsider can be a useful resource to families facing important inflection points in their respective life cycles.

The chapter title should help you figure out where we are going next. Depending on how old you are, you may have different views on just what a coach is and what a coach does.

Generational Divide

My experience is that the older someone is, the less likely they are to "get" what coaching is. I'll give you two examples.

In the first years after the turn of the 21st century, a member of my family was considering a career change, and he was seriously looking into the field of coaching. My opinion is that this person would have been a great coach. Unfortunately, he decided to ask my dad for advice on this move.

My dad was a very smart and successful self-made man, and once he got even an inkling of an idea in his head, it was usually difficult to get him to see any other point of view. I was not present during the conversation when my relative asked for Dad's advice, but I distinctly recall Dad relaying his views in the following days.

He questioned why anyone would want to make a career out of "helping losers." To him, anyone who needed to talk to someone to help them figure things out, set priorities and be held accountable was someone who fell into the loser category.

Let's just say that the coaching industry has made huge strides in credibility in the past couple of decades, but my dad likely never would have been a fan.

In my second example, a few years ago I became aware of a family in which the patriarch was beginning to experience the effects of dementia, and his four offspring were wondering how they should deal with the new reality that they would be called on to make decisions. (I use "offspring" rather than "children" because "children" makes one think of youngsters who still need to be looked after. Some of my colleagues use "former children," but that might make you wonder if they somehow divorced themselves from the family.)

At the suggestion of someone from their bank, the family considered hiring an outsider to work with the four siblings to help them prepare for the future in a harmonious way. There had been a liquidity event over a decade before and lots of tax-saving tactics had been implemented since, but the four were largely in the dark about the family finances and could certainly have benefitted from an independent outsider working with them to figure out how to proceed.

I know the family and the prospective coach they interviewed. Unfortunately I also know they did not hire this person, in part because the patriarch got hung up on one word. "Why would we need a coach?" he asked. Apparently, he also made a remark about not being a hockey team.

In both examples, the person who didn't "get" coaching was someone born in the 1930s.

Murray Bowen on Coaching

Now just to disprove my point, I want to talk about Murray Bowen and how he viewed coaching. Try to ignore the fact that

Bowen was born in 1913. He really was ahead of his time and probably a freak of nature in many ways, so we will grant him an exemption from my theory about age and understanding the value of coaching. Bowen liked to call himself a coach when he was working with colleagues who had accepted his challenge of working with members of their family of origin.

Recall our earlier discussion in which I used the swimming analogy. Bowen strongly encouraged his students to experience the work of getting in touch with as many members of their family of origin as possible, and to work on their own differentiation of self by doing so. He had figured out for himself the value in getting to a point where each of his one-on-one relationships with family members was as objective as possible.

He also recognized that getting to that point is almost always much more difficult than it sounds, and that anyone who is serious about it will need to reflect on the process and hopefully will have someone who can talk them through it and keep them on track. Bowen liked the term "coaching" for this type of work with other therapists who were working on their own differentiation efforts. He also talked about working with young adults with the goal of coaching them in "differentiating a self from their family of origin."

Coaching a Family

When a family is working on the details of transitioning their wealth from the current generation of leaders to the one that will eventually take their place, plenty of situations will arise that could benefit from the perspective and input of an objective outsider.

We've already mentioned many of the various professional advisors who bring their own particular expertise. These specialists are usually from outside the system, which is a plus.

Some of them also hold themselves out as resources for the family, especially as it pertains to explaining the work they have done on behalf of the family.

In some cases these advisors are more than adequate for the task at hand, and it is often worth trying them out as a first step, if everyone is willing to give it a go. Often, however, whether due to the size of the family or its complexity, or the fact that there are already some obviously touchy subjects to deal with, it is better to look for someone who is trained specifically in dealing with family interactions.

No Stake in the Solution

One of the problems that can arise when the family simply asks their estate-planning lawyer to run the family meeting to explain the transition plan is that the lawyer has a vested interest in coming out of it with their hard work intact. If I have spent months working on something with the parents and now have to present it as a fait accompli to the kids, there is a pretty strong likelihood that I am going to get a bit defensive when anyone questions my work.

Contrast that scenario with an independent, unbiased outsider who has been hired to facilitate a session to discuss the estate plan. This person was not involved in the preparation of the plans being presented, and as a facilitator, their job is to make sure the discussion is productive and civilized. The root of the word facilitator, facile, is French for "easy" – their job is to make things easier.

Facilitator versus Coach. And What about Mediation?

We have now crossed over into the sometimes arcane world of defining job descriptions and titles. I have personally spent what feels like too much time on this subject in my own life, and from speaking with colleagues I know I am not alone.

Definitions are flexible and we use words in ways that work for us. It would be nice if there were standard definitions for these terms but I'm not sure there will be agreement anytime soon. My personal view is that **coaching** is usually a one-on-one process, while groups of people typically call for **facilitation**. Many people still call it coaching even when one coach works with a group.

The expression "when you move from your seat to your feet" describes another way to know when you've moved from coaching to facilitation. Facilitation usually involves movement, even if it's only to get up to write things on a flip chart.

As long as we are addressing roles and titles, we should touch on mediation here too, if only because I have included "mediator" on my business card for years.

Despite the fact that one family matriarch hired me to be the "referee" for their family meetings, I think mediator is a better fit. **Mediation** is a formalized process whereby each party is invited to make their points of view and concerns heard, and the mediator works with them to attempt to find enough common ground to arrive at a mutually acceptable solution.

When I started my mediation training, I had recently completed a series of coaching training workshops, and I can tell you I was glad I had done the training in that order. The skills one learns in coaching are instantly applicable for many mediation scenarios, especially learning to listen.

The Evolution of Coaching

The coaching profession continues to evolve and become more accepted in society. With this success have come some growing pains, not the least of which is the fact that anyone can call themselves a coach without much regulation. As with hiring anyone, it behooves you to take the time to ask lots of questions, check references and do some basic research online to see what you can learn about anyone before you hire them to work with your family.

The fields of family business and family wealth continue to evolve as well, and people who work with families from these domains now have a variety of ways to get trained in the important specifics that these clients require.

Considerations for families

Many families could certainly benefit from working with a coach or facilitator. Families that have attained a certain level of wealth usually have a lot at stake when it comes to finding the best way to transition that wealth to the next generation. My opinion is that families with a lot to lose should try to do whatever is necessary to minimize the risk of making a big mistake with this important work.

Can your other outside experts really do the job that is required to get the entire family on board? Are they trained for this part, and do they want to do it? Can they do it well enough?

Considerations for motivated individuals in the family

There is often one person who sees the need to bring in a coach to work with the family.

As we saw in the examples at the beginning of this chapter, it may make sense for the prospective coach to use other words to describe their services because hiring a "coach" may not resonate with everyone, especially those who likely hold a veto.

If you are the individual reaching out to a coach or facilitator to work with your family, make sure that anyone you bring in takes the time to work with you to figure out the best way for them to be introduced to the rest of the family so that you maximize the chances of success. Anyone who tries to muscle past you and go straight to the parents, thinking that is the best way in, is probably not the right person to hire.

Considerations for advisors to families

If you work with families that have attained significant wealth, and you sometimes feel like you are beyond your comfort zone when it comes time to work with all of the family members, you could likely benefit from aligning yourself with someone who can join you for important family meetings.

Surely most of your family clients are ones that you will be able to continue to take care of from A to Z, at least most of the time. But when it comes to more complex families, or families in which the parents are even a bit concerned with how the planning will affect family relationships, it is probably well worth it for you to have some outside resources that you can bring in to support you in the area of family dynamics.

Interdependent Wealth

CHAPTER 7. HOW CAN'T I HELP YOU?

When speaking with wealth creators, a common theme runs through their stories. Through hard work, determination, risk-taking, some luck and maybe even divine intervention, they made it big and were eventually in a position to offer their family a much easier life than their middle- or working class – or even hand to mouth – beginnings offered.

What a fantastic reward for all that effort.

I Don't Want That for My Kids

One part of the story that wealth creators often seem to miss is how important their starting circumstances may have been in their success. Necessity may be the mother of invention, but it's also a key ingredient in the drive that many people have.

While the tough times were tough, and it's easy to understand why any loving parent would want to spare their children the worst parts, is it possible to make things too easy for our kids? To help them too much? Um, yes. And it happens all the time.

In the developed world, parents from most social strata are confronted very early with the many choices they must make in raising their children. Many of the decisions come down to finding the balance between providing for their children's needs and spoiling them by giving them too much.

I mentioned "most" social strata rather than "all" because at the subsistence level, parents struggle just to supply the bare minimum, so their opportunities to spoil their children are much rarer. But what about the other end of the wealth spectrum? When you can literally afford to give your children anything and everything, where do you stop? Where should you stop?

What Is Too Much Help?

Society changes with each generation, of course, and it can be difficult to raise a family "differently" in a society where it seems like all parents are doing things a certain way. Sometimes you know it doesn't feel right but you get carried away with a desire to go along to get along.

Do you really want to fight the fight about the Tooth Fairy giving your kids the same $5 per tooth that the other kids in the neighbourhood are getting? Maybe you do and maybe you don't; either way is fine. I simply want to illustrate some of the mundane, day-to-day stuff that comes up.

I won't even get into the situations where each parent has a different view on how much to provide, because that's enough to write a whole other book about. Luckily, my wife and I never really had any huge differences of opinion in these areas when we were raising our two children, so thankfully I never developed much expertise in that arena.

I hope I've begun to lay out a case for the fact that sometimes too much help can be a problem. I'm also reasonably certain that everyone reading this could provide a number of real-life examples from their own lives. What I'm saying is that situations where someone is helping too much, and therefore someone else is being helped too much, are something we have all probably noticed. But I wonder how easy it is to notice these situations when we are one of the parties involved, as opposed to an outsider.

Getting Too Much Help

When you receive a lot of help from someone, it can become difficult to admit it. Sometimes you barely notice it because you take it for granted and then begin to rationalize it: "Mom has always made my lunch. I told her to stop but she won't. Oh well; it makes her happy, so I let her."

That's a situation that is relatively benign on the surface, and nobody is being hurt by it, so what's the big deal? It is also a great example of interdependence, or reciprocity. Each person gets something out of it. I'm sure there are plenty of people on the receiving end of help in situations akin to this one who would hesitate to admit they are getting too much help. But many outsiders would be able to spot it 100 yards away.

Giving Too Much Help

If it's difficult to admit when we get too much help, how about those on the other side, the ones who give too much? My gut tells me these people have even more difficulty recognizing this trait in themselves. Especially when we are talking about parents doing things for their children, it can be next to impossible to see these over-helping situations for what they really are.

At the risk of overstating the case, I think most cases of parents doing too much for their children are more about the parents wanting to feel good about themselves than they are about the children really needing the help.

Let's go back to Mom making lunch for her son. Now think about it at various ages and stages of life. When the boy is 5 years old, nobody has a problem with it. At 15, some would say it's a bit much, but would still be alright with it. When he's 25 it is starting to be pretty weird, and at 35 we can assume the son has given up.

Unfortunately, the 35-year-old probably hasn't just given up the fight with Mom about making his lunch, he has also likely given up a bunch of other things in this relationship that have clearly outlasted the natural arc of mother-son interactions.

But does Mom see it the same way? She's just helping, because she loves him!

The Family Systems View

Recall that when we are trying to think "systems," it is less about the people themselves and more about the relationships between the people. Of course those relationships typically function best when the people are all operating at the same level.

What do I mean by "level"? Let's start by thinking of a group of people who are at a relatively homogenous level – say, a first-year undergraduate college class. The teacher at the front of the room can assume that everyone in the class is qualified to be there and can teach them as if they are equal.

Let's contrast that to the one-room schoolhouse, where the teacher has a room full of all the kids in town, including two first-graders, four second-graders, three from third grade, and so on. This teacher needs to adapt a teaching style that incorporates methods of dealing with various levels of people who are all trying to learn, in the same room at the same time.

Now let's think about a family situation, and to make it easier, all the offspring are adults. The ideal scenario with parents and adult offspring would be akin to the undergraduate class – everyone is treated as if they are on the same level. But I am sure many readers know of families in which an adult gathering is anything but a group of equals.

Whether it is because a parent is an autocratic leader, or because one of the offspring never quite grew up and "launched" into adulthood, or for a myriad of other possible reasons (or excuses), the gathering doesn't remotely resemble a meeting of people on the same level.

These kinds of family situations usually include some members who see themselves as "one up" – that is, above some or all of the others – as well as some who are "one down," feeling they are below others. The one-ups usually think they are helping the group with their "superior" ideas and input, while the one-downs have usually resigned themselves to positions of helplessness.

A group of related people will behave as a system, and that system will try to find equilibrium. That equilibrium can be maintained for months, years, even decades.

Time Catches Up

Just as we progressively added 10 years in our lunch-making example, let's do it with a member of the leading generation. Let's use an autocratic figure called "Dad."

When Dad is 60 and he tries to control his 30-something offspring, it may still fly. When Dad is 70, he may begin to lose his fastball.

When Dad is 80, my guess is that the 50-something children will be quite tired of his game and will recognize that time is on their side. Most dads who reach 90 will not be the alpha male any longer. The earlier Dad recognizes that his "advantage" is only temporary, the better. At some point he will need to rely on those offspring that he was controlling to take care of day-to-day activities and decisions he is no longer capable of taking care of himself.

Who is going to help him when he needs it?

Imbalances Abound

As I work with families who have concerns about transitioning their wealth from the current generation to the ones that follow, situations with people on different levels come up all the time. Ideally, when everyone is an adult, they should be able to have adult-to-adult discussions about things that are important to all of them. This is not always the case, however.

Family discussions often continue to occur with big imbalances between generations or among members of a generation. And there are usually some members who think that nothing would ever get done without their help.

My Kingdom for a Resource: Avoiding Intrusive Helpfulness

One day I was on a coaching call with a Bowen coach and I was telling her about a situation involving my wife and her family. I told her that I could see some areas where my wife's family could use my help, and that I wanted to help.

Then came the ah-ha moment. A great coach usually makes their biggest mark not with a statement, but with a question. The coach said, "What if you didn't help your wife? What if you were just a resource for her?"

At this point she could have dropped the proverbial mic, because I was dumbstruck.

The coach didn't use the term "intrusive helpfulness" at the time, but that's definitely what she was encouraging me to stop offering.

After our call, I went to my wife and told her that I wasn't going to help her with her family situation anymore. She gave me a quizzical look, and said, "Okay…," waiting for the punchline.

I couldn't leave her hanging so I added, "But if you ever need me as a resource, I will always be there for you."

Since that time, I have tried to banish the word "help" from my vocabulary. So much helping is "one-up" helping, where the helper sees themself as a rescuer of someone who would be helpless without them.

As we discussed at the beginning of this chapter, making things too easy for people doesn't usually end up being helpful because they never learn to be self-reliant.

Considerations for families

If you are part of a family in which there are adults who are constantly "helping" and others who are constantly "being helped," the first step is to recognize the situation. Until people recognize the situation, they are not likely to change anything. Recognizing the problem is only the first step, but it is an important one.

If nobody is motivated to change the situation, the equilibrium will remain, but as soon as even one person is ready to make some changes, some movement can begin.

Considerations for motivated individuals in the family

You need to remember that in a system, the members are constantly reacting to each other, and they will try to maintain the equilibrium. If you want things to change, you need to change yourself and you need to be able to stand firm and hold on to the change you are hoping to make; otherwise, the forces that maintain the old equilibrium will outlast you.

State your "I-Position" and stick with it, despite what others say or threaten to do.

Considerations for advisors to families

As an advisor to a family, you are likely in a great position to notice situations where there is too much helping going on.

It is not always easy to talk to your clients about these personal matters, which can include questioning some of their parenting choices and skills. Most advisors will therefore not venture into these areas, and that's too bad. These wealthy clients already have so many "yes men" in their lives that they are often crying out for someone to tell them the important truths they just aren't seeing.

Interdependent Wealth

Interdependent Wealth

CHAPTER 8. INFORMAL CONNECTIONS

We've just completed a chapter in which we looked at the relationships in a family group, while noting some of the ways in which not everyone may be on the same level, along with some of the problems that can cause.

At some point, it becomes important to create some formal structures and rules for how everyone needs to behave to work together properly. This aspect of family relations is nicely summed up by one of my favourite expressions: "formality is your friend."

But we aren't going there just yet, because we first need to spend some time looking at the informal connections in family groups – and the roles they play.

Informality Is Everywhere

I want to begin with a flashback of my own life and early career, so I'll ask you to please join me in the late 1980s. I was in my early 20s at the time, and I had just completed my Bachelor's degree at McGill University in Montreal. I had studied business because it had been made clear to me over the past couple of decades that my destiny was to eventually take over the company my dad had started.

I had a title, which I believe was marketing manager. We really didn't have a marketing department, so it was a safe place to stick me without stepping on anyone's toes and still had me reporting directly to the "Big Guy," as we referred to my dad (although never in his presence!).

I spent much of my workday wandering around to the various departments to inquire what was going on and to learn how things operated. Very little of what I did was "formal" in any sense of the word. It was my own on-the-job training and I was figuring it out on the fly.

I was driven by my own curiosity and my sense that it was good for me to understand all aspects of the business since I would someday need to know how everything worked. I was able to do this successfully for a couple of reasons. Number one was the fact that my dad owned the place, so nobody ever felt like they could kick me out of their office. I'm pretty sure he never explicitly told anyone they needed to indulge my visits and questions, they just knew it.

But the number two reason this worked was that I did it in a completely non-threatening way. In retrospect, I'm pretty sure that my approach was successful largely because curiosity was my biggest driver.

MBWA

Around that time, one of the biggest business books of the decade was showing up on bestseller lists. I picked up a copy of In Search of Excellence and read it with interest. I had a business degree and was preparing to eventually run a business, so I was anxious to learn anything and everything that might help me do it well.

Imagine my pleasant surprise when I read the part about MBWA.

While I had been going from one department head's office to another and making myself at home and asking lots of questions, part of me actually felt a bit guilty: This didn't seem like a "real job" in any way, because I was actually enjoying it.

Then one evening while reading In Search of Excellence, I got to the chapter espousing the merits of MBWA.

Oh my God!

Management by Wandering Around was actually written about in this bestselling book as a great way to lead and know what is going on! At the time I had not realized it, because I just did what seemed natural given my curiosity and my long-term goal of understanding everything, but what I was really doing was nurturing the informal relationships I would need to rely on.

Business versus Family

Of course the relationships I'm talking about cultivating were mostly business relationships, although one of the department heads was my cousin and another was my uncle. And of course my dad was everyone's ultimate boss, so I was afforded more deference than any other 20-something kid who might wander into an office and start asking questions.

When you consider family relationships, at first glance you might assume that informal relationships would be easier, because of the family bond. On the other hand, when you get into sensitive subjects where discussions can veer over to money, self-worth and even death, well, sometimes people can be too close for comfort.

So let's refresh our memories about what it means to take a systems view of things. A system of people who are related is more about the relationships between the people than it is about the people themselves. One of the ways I like to think of this is to imagine a piece of paper with four dots on it, where the dots each represent a person. Now draw lines to connect all of the dots. Systems thinking is more about the lines and less about the dots.

Formal versus Informal

When we think about the relationships we have in our lives, most of them are usually pretty informal. From an early age, when we first went to school, our parents surely signed some forms for us to be there and the school put us in a certain classroom, but our interactions with other kids, the school employees and the bus driver all just sort of happened, often anonymously.

In fact, when we end up with lots of formal relationships, it usually isn't a good thing. I'm thinking police officers, judges, and parole officers here. Much of our success in life comes down to how we handle ourselves in our informal relationships.

Family Wealth and Its Governance

As I noted at the beginning of this chapter, however, there is a time when "formality is your friend" can become an important rallying cry. Sometimes just by virtue of the amount of wealth that is at stake, it behooves a family to formalize how they are handling their wealth, now and for the future.

Having some formality becomes most important when one generation of the family is controlling the wealth and they are preparing to move that control to the succeeding generation.

An underlying complicating factor that sometimes may not even be noticed is that this stage also often coincides with the move from a more centralized autocratic decision-making style to a more collegial group that is expected to decide things together. In that setting, it becomes more important to make sure that all stakeholders clearly understand what is at stake and how they are going to go about their work together.

But remember in the last chapter when we talked about the fact that not everyone is operating at the same level? That reality rears its head in this sandbox too.

Formal Structures, Informal Leadership

While there is a real need for some formal structures and procedures to properly govern family wealth, we aren't necessarily looking at using parliamentary procedures or Robert's Rules of Order. In fact, when a family can find the right balance of formality of procedures and informality of leadership, it can be a beautiful thing.

Of course, the better people know each other and get along informally – that is, outside the formal governance process – the smoother the meetings about formal governance are likely to be. This is probably true for both family and non-family groups working together in any capacity.

Doing Your Own Bowen Work

As we now move to where Bowen Family Systems Theory comes into play, I must confess that I'm not necessarily going to cite a lot in Murray Bowen's writings here.

Earlier, I mentioned that there is kind of an assumption that serious Bowen students will not simply learn about what Bowen was studying and preaching, but also undertake much of the important "self-work" that is required to be a true "Bowenite." It is in this part of the BFST work that I have found the strongest connection to the other matters I've been discussing in this chapter. Those who really buy into the study of BFST understand that living it is more about being (who you are) than simply doing (what you do).

Bowen himself encouraged his students to continue to work on their own differentiation of self. One of the main ways to do that is to continuously work on any unresolved emotional attachment to one's family of origin. And the best way to do that is to work on developing as many connections as possible to as many members of one's extended family as possible.

Having been involved with other trainees at the Bowen Center in our small afternoon consultation groups, I cannot count how many far-ranging genograms I saw drawn on the blackboard (including my own). Our coach was always asking about some great uncle or third cousin we may want to try to contact.

Sometimes it almost felt like we were being encouraged to be in contact with as many people in our family tree as possible – quantity at the cost of quality – but I know that was not the point. But if you had the choice of having one very strong relationship or a handful of adult-to-adult connections, there are good reasons to believe that the latter would serve you better in the long run.

Revisiting the individual–togetherness spectrum, the feeling is that the more options you have for people in your family to speak to about any concern or question, the better. But notice that none of these relationships or connections are really formal in any way. It is more about being on good terms with people and having a fresh enough contact with them that reaching out to them doesn't feel odd or uncomfortable. I know this is often a problem with contacting distant family members and can be an excuse not to do so. "They'll think it's weird, and wonder what I want" is a sentiment that comes up frequently.

Bowen trainees are encouraged to silence those thoughts and persevere. And with social media and email, it is much easier to stay in touch today than when letters, phone calls and visits were the only options.

Not Looking for Help

One of the reasons that developing this large family network of connections is seen as so important is that a lot of potential strength can be garnered from a family's human capital. You won't necessarily be asking these extended family members for "help" per se, but you may be able to call on them as a resource someday.

The more adult-to-adult relationships you have within a family, without either side being one up or one down, the better you can relate to each other and see your relationship as simply a connection of equals in which one is as likely to be the resource as the other.

The more connections like this a family can have, the more people can relate to each other without taking sides or feeling stuck or caught in an uncomfortable situation. The informal connections are what we should all be striving for.

Considerations for families

Families that don't have many get-togethers are at a bit of a disadvantage here. Some family leaders really need to make the effort to create opportunities for large groups of family members to come together. Of course when someone invites people to something, there is a need for the people to actually show up; otherwise there will not be a lot of progress.

For families with wealth who have never called a family meeting, it would be wise to start small and informally first before tackling serious subjects. The more the family can learn to function well together without any pressure to make any big decisions, the better.

Considerations for motivated individuals in the family

If you are the one in the family who knows you all need more informal interactions, bravo. Start small and aim for progress, not perfection. Putting pressure on people to attend a get-together can often backfire, so try to avoid that. It's better to have a small event everyone actually wants to attend than a large one where some people need to be dragged in kicking and screaming.

The goal should never be to have one big event, but rather to begin a series of get-togethers where the family can learn to work together and be civil and productive.

Considerations for advisors to families

This isn't a natural place for advisors to get involved with families, except perhaps to highlight some of the points in this chapter and how important it is for any family to have events where people come together just for the sake of spending time together and deepening their relationships.

If you are convening a big family meeting for a client family, you may want to ask how often this group gets together less formally. At least the answer to that question will help you be properly prepared.

Interdependent Wealth

Interdependent Wealth

CHAPTER 9. LEADERSHIP

Having just looked at the importance of informal connections, we have now arrived in a new place, one that has a much more common name: leadership.

Leadership is a word (and a subject) that everyone has heard, and most people have their own understanding of what it is and what it looks like. Despite the variety of definitions and examples, though, I think most people do get the fact that great leadership is pretty important and that projects and efforts with great leaders will always have a greater chance of success than ones where leadership is poor or non-existent.

Family Wealth Leadership

In just about every wealthy family I've ever heard of, there has been plenty of evidence of great leadership involved in the creation and growth of the wealth. It almost goes without saying that wealth creation, at least before the advent of huge Mega Millions and Powerball lotteries, always involves some extraordinary ability, effort, risk-taking and luck – and the leadership necessary to put it all together.

Maybe you've heard the old saw about the fact that it's easier to get rich than to stay rich, and I can surely buy that argument. To extend that idea, I'd say it's easier to create the initial wealth than it is to successfully transition that wealth to successive generations of one's family. If that were not at least partly true, this book would not exist.

In my first book, SHIFT Your Family Business: Stop Working IN Your Family Business and Start Working ON Your Business Family, I spent a lot of time discussing the fact that it is important for the family leader to make that shift at some point.

For years (and likely decades), the focus was on the business or the wealth and on growing it at all costs. The wealth creation machine that is the business can be all-consuming, and many other concerns can be put aside while the focus is on making the proverbial pie bigger.

Eventually, though, and hopefully before it is too late, someone will realize there is an important family element that can no longer be forced to play second fiddle. Somewhere in the family leadership hierarchy, often with both parents, the idea of focusing on the business first and the family second will become a red flag.

Once the family leaders recognize that it is more useful to think of themselves as a business family, some important steps can begin to happen.

Business Leader and Family Leader

Let's start by recognizing that the business will always require great leadership. But let's also acknowledge that the family needs its own great leadership. Is that one leader with two hats, or two different leaders?

Great question. I hope you don't expect me to give you "the" answer. But if you force me to, my answer will be a simple "yes."

Yes, it is one leader with two hats, and yes, it can be two different leaders. And over time and depending on other family life cycle circumstances, leadership will likely shift back and forth between the two scenarios. The most important thing to realize is that both the business and the family require leadership, and that insofar as it is possible, this leadership question should be addressed explicitly.

Family Leader as Family Champion

As family wealth is expected to go from Generation 1 to Generation 2, and eventually to G3, G4, etc., a lot of other changes are going on as well. The family tree is likely growing with more and more branches, making the picture more complex. At the same time, the simple fact that we are talking about whole generations, going from G1 to G3 or G2 to G4, means several decades are involved; where each person is in their individual life cycle will necessarily change quite drastically during that time.

This combination of adding people to the mix and these people each advancing in their own timelines makes the entire subject of wealth transition a huge dynamic moving target. What is often needed to hold it all together is a person who steps forward to act as a "family champion."

Once a family has successfully arrived at, say, G3 or G4, there will often be some formal governance structures in place, which may include a family council, for example. But when you are going from G1 to G2 and no formal structures exist yet, it usually takes one motivated individual to step up, often quietly at first, and assume the informal role of family champion.

As the wealth is expected to serve successive generations, there really needs to be some family leadership in each generation, but the toughest transition is usually from G1 to G2, because there is no model to follow.

The whole concept of being a business family instead of a family business is usually a whole new idea for people to try to understand. And unless the family also knows other families in similar circumstances or deals with advisors who have been around this block, many of these ideas will sound foreign and be hard to grasp.

Leadership Traits

Any person who hopes to have success as a family system leader will ideally have a few particular things going for them, because while it may sound simple, there are more ways to do it wrong than there are to get it right.

First of all, the family system does not exist in a vacuum, because the business system or the wealth usually casts a pretty big shadow. The business system leaders will have become used to holding the dominant position and any family issues will usually be considered of secondary importance. So the family leader will need to be patient and be okay with quiet leadership. They will also have to content themselves with doing much of their thinking, worrying and planning by themselves – the CEO of the business will have a personal assistant and several department heads to rely on; the family leader will typically be flying solo.

Along with patience and the ability to forge ahead alone, the family leader will need to be able to continuously work informally with all stakeholders, because in the end, they will want to represent the widest possible set of ideas, questions and priorities the family has.

If you've ever known someone who ran a successful business and then moved into the non-profit sector, you've likely heard about how much more difficult leadership is in their new domain. Whereas they used to be able to command people to do things with the implicit threat that they could be fired, now they are suddenly working with many volunteers, so that threat is now gone, and in many ways almost reversed!

That's part of the reality of the family champion too. There are no levers of power. In fact, until the champion works their influence up to a certain level, there isn't really any power at all.

Systems View

As we move into the world of systems theory, recall that any one person is simply that: one person in a system that includes many other people. The other people are individual points in the system, and it's really only possible to change yourself and the way you relate to the other people in the system. You cannot directly change anyone else, except to the extent that they will adjust in response to how you alter the way you relate to them.

One of the ways a leader can get others to follow them is to model the kind of behaviour they believe others should adopt. Murray Bowen had a different way of talking about this, and it goes far beyond simple modelling. He liked to talk about the I-Position, which I mentioned earlier.

The I-Position may be one of the best-kept secrets of BFST, if you ask me. And you're reading my book, so it's like you asked me.

Taking an I-Position is part of the process of differentiation of self. You are defining, first for yourself and then for others, what you will do and what you will not do. These decisions about what you will and won't do should come after plenty of reflection around your own values and grounding principles. As a leader, you need to base your actions on the ideas that are most important to you, and the clearer and more consistent you can be on the details, the better.

A person desiring to be a family leader will usually hold to principles that include the importance of the family as a focal point for all decisions and actions taken with the business and the wealth.

But recall the part about being patient and strong and often going it alone. It can be lonely, and there will be some family members who don't care about the family very much and think the whole family element just makes their job more difficult. Strong family leaders must resist members of the system who don't agree with the family leader and who expect the leader to eventually get tired of the battle and give up.

The business system likely has strong leaders. For a family to successfully transition its wealth to following generations, the family system needs strong leadership too.

Considerations for families

If the family has not yet had a successful wealth transition because G1 leadership is still concentrating on making the business bigger, you may want to think about the simple question of the difference between a family business and a business family as part of a thought-provoking discussion.

If the family has already survived one intergenerational transition, that's a great start. There is often a decades-long gap between the first such transition and the next. But is it time to start planning the next one? Later ones are "easier" because you all know it needs to happen, but usually they are actually more difficult because typically, more people are involved.

Getting the discussions started early will give you more time to get everyone involved and to get everything just right.

Considerations for motivated individuals in the family

If you are motivated to act because you see that something needs to be done, congratulations – you have family leadership potential. The desire to act is often more important than having the required skills. Skills can be learned; motivation is more difficult to instill. Start thinking about the principles on which you will base your I-Positions.

Considerations for advisors to families

If you have clients who need to think about their transitions, usually the best thing you can do for them is to continue to bring up the subject. They may get sick of hearing it, but you need to continue to mention it. Remind them that starting early gives them the most options and that waiting until the last minute never leads to better decisions.

You can also tell them that you would like to be a resource for them as they tackle this project.

Interdependent Wealth

CHAPTER 10. PEER LEARNING

As we leave the chapter on leadership, we won't let it get too far behind us. If you are working on transitioning family wealth, the subject of leadership is never really far away, is it? We are now moving on to another interesting subject, which in many ways will take us outside the realm of our own family: peer learning.

Let me start by explaining what I mean by peer learning, because while it may be very obvious to some people, for others it may be quite foreign. And I have a sneaking suspicion that for some family business people in particular, it will be completely counter to their standard ways of operating.

Peer Learning in a Nutshell

Peer learning involves finding people outside your organization who are going through situations and challenges similar to yours, and getting together regularly to share experiences and ideas for mutual benefit.

I will start with a couple of examples from earlier in my own career and expand from there. In the 1980s, the Canadian Association of Family Enterprise (CAFE) was created as a place where family businesses could learn from each other. While it had symposia and local chapters in various cities across Canada, my dad joined and got the most value out of its personal advisory groups (PAGs).

When you joined CAFE, you were encouraged to join a local PAG, where you were put into a group of 8 to 10 other family business members who were in positions similar to yours (CEOs with CEOs, next-gen members with other next-gen members, etc.). Great care was taken to make sure there were no business competitors in a PAG, and confidentiality was always encouraged and reinforced.

Dad used to really look forward to these get-togethers with his "buddy group," and the PAG members sort of became each other's informal advisory boards. Running a business can be pretty lonely, and even tougher when it's a family business, so becoming close to others who are truly peers can be very helpful.

While CAFE also provided a facilitator to help organize the group and get them moving in the right direction within a framework, eventually my dad's official PAG ceased to exist. But the core group continued to get together. Even after most of them had sold their businesses or retired, they continued to have an annual holiday lunch together. The peer learning continued.

Soon after my dad passed away, his old buddy group invited me to join them for that lunch one year, and it was great to swap old stories with people who had great memories of my old man.

Learning a New Industry

Since we are back in the 1980s, I'll share another example of peer learning that was part of my formative training.
The main business of our family company was steel fabrication, which was pretty much all we did for the first two decades. But most of the steel we were fabricating needed to be hot-dip galvanized before we sent it to our customers for assembly and installation. Galvanizing was a huge cost and an extra hassle for us because we didn't have that capability in-house. So eventually we expanded into the galvanizing business, which was a whole new world for us.

One of the first moves my dad made was to join the American Hot Dip Galvanizers' Association (AHDGA). He started to go to its meetings, which often included plant visits to others in the business in cities across North America. He explained to me that when you are new at something, the best thing you can do is to find others who know about the subject and learn from them. But of course you cannot just "take" as a member of any peer group. Within a few short years, other members of AHDGA were regularly visiting our galvanizing plant and we shared the ways we were doing things with them as well. What goes around comes around.

The Bowen Trainee Version

I wish I could tell you that a similar, easily accessible network existed for people who want to learn about Bowen Family Systems Theory from each other. I'm not saying that nothing exists anywhere for people who want to share Bowen stuff and learn from each other, but such groups are certainly not prevalent or easy to find, in my experience. But that doesn't mean there's no hope, either.

Before I get ahead of myself, I need to explain the ways in which peer learning have been instrumental in my increasing exposure to and comfort with everything related to the world and work of Murray Bowen. When I began my formal Bowen training in Vermont it was via a grassroots effort by a couple of local Bowen aficionados who decided to put together a program based on the one they had attended at Georgetown.

I say "grassroots" because in many ways these were simply Bowen peers who wanted to expose the ideas to more people. They wanted to share their knowledge and experience to expand the network of people who can confidently learn and use the theory that Bowen created and worked hard at popularizing.

After a couple of years of that, having decided that I was indeed hell-bent on writing a book about Bowen Theory and its application to the world of transitioning family wealth, I decided to kick things up a notch, and I applied to the post-graduate program at the Bowen Center in DC.

I'm not sure what I expected to find there, but it wasn't that much different from Vermont. Sure, it was more established, having been created and set up by Dr. Bowen himself. The Center had its own facilities, including classrooms, meeting rooms and offices.

The faculty of a dozen or so people came into the classroom at different points along the way to talk about specific subjects that reflected their expertise and interests. One of the most fascinating things for me, though, was that the organizational structure was quite flat – the people running everything essentially treated each other as peers. Not only that, during the afternoon "supervision" or consultation sessions, where we broke into small groups with one coach/leader, much of the learning was also peer-to-peer.

Sharing Stories and Learning Together

Those sessions were essentially an opportunity to share something from our own family or a client family and to talk about it in question-and-answer fashion with the coach. A trainee would do this for about 45 minutes or so with the coach, and the other trainees observed. I was lucky to have a great coach from whom I learned a great deal, just by watching. I can only assume that the other coaches were also great teachers.

While the faculty members and coaches were all experienced and got to their positions through merit, the vast majority of them always came across to me as peers. There was not a lot of pontificating from on high. It felt like everyone was there to try to learn this stuff together, with each other and from each other. Based on the many videotapes of Dr. Bowen that we watched, it seems that this was part of the culture he had instilled in the place.

There's an old adage that the best way to learn something is to teach it to someone else, because to do that, you must force yourself to really understand the subject. (The same thing can be said for writing a book, but I digress).

The Bowen world also contains a loose network of people who get together for conferences a couple of times a year, organized by the Bowen Center, although networking has not seemed to be a high priority.

Recall the individual–togetherness continuum that is basic to Bowen Theory. Bowen and his early disciples seemed to think it was important to try to force people to move towards the individual end of the spectrum, because there is a natural tendency for people to take the easier route and congregate on the togetherness end. This mindset has created a culture in which people at the Bowen Center lean towards self-sufficiency and self-reflection, at a time when much of the rest of the world is trying to find ways to reap the benefits of sharing.

I think this may be changing, however. I personally believe that for Bowen Theory to become more widespread, more peer learning opportunities will have to be part of the plan.

Family Members as Peers

So far in this chapter we've looked at ways to learn from peers in the outside world – that is, non-family members. But the focus of this book is intergenerational wealth transitions, which naturally means we are going to be thinking about family members working together.

Where does the "peer learning" come into play there? I'm glad you asked. Let's start by going back to the basic definition of a system –in this case, the family system. A peer is another member of a system. But we have never discussed any hierarchy in the systems we've been talking about.

Of course every family will have some sort of hierarchy consisting of the different generations, and maybe other hierarchies due to birth order or even gender. Some families get really hung up on their hierarchies, especially when those in the senior positions are desperately trying to retain the upper hand.

I know that in many business families, there is a tendency for those who work in the business to maintain an air of superiority over those who don't, and to want to maintain control of their positional power. Other family members who do not happen to be working in the business are much less informed about the business's goings on and are sometimes treated as a nuisance by those who feel like they are doing all the work while others are benefitting from it as family owners.

Situations where this is the prevalent attitude are fraught with difficulty when it comes time to transition the business and wealth to the rising generation. All family members are stakeholders in the business or wealth, even those who don't work in the business or have anything to do with managing the wealth.

And yes, even those who are not owners are also stakeholders, including those who will never be owners. They are still part of the system, and so they are stakeholders who cannot be ignored. Well, strictly speaking you can ignore them, but you do so at your peril.

The more you can create a system in which family members treat each other as peers, the better. If you think I am talking about siblings and cousins here you are correct. But even when it comes to relationships between members of one generation and another, the same applies, even if it can be more difficult to get there.

The name of this book is Interdependent Wealth, and you should never forget that interdependence involves give and take. It may be difficult to fathom for those who are in the control positions now, but no position is eternal. If you are a leader, you were once a follower; other leaders will take their turns, and you will possibly be a follower again.

Families that have already been through this cycle at least once have the advantage of knowing how it works in practice. The current generation can learn from what their forebears went through as part of their transition. The sooner everyone realizes they are peers, and begins to act like it, the smoother the transitions will go.

Considerations for families

If you haven't looked for any outside peer learning opportunities, you are probably missing out. Some families seem to be reluctant to go outside the family for learning, fearing that others cannot be trusted. That attitude often causes more problems than it solves. Feeling that you are the only person facing a problem can be lonely. Finding others who are going through similar situations can be very liberating.
If your family is still very hierarchical, you likely have your work cut out for you to get everyone to act more like peers. But this change can start as soon as those at the top realize it is in their long-term interest to change their attitude.

Considerations for motivated individuals in the family

Getting other family members on board with your way of seeing things can be a long road. But if you persist, and gradually get more and more people on side, you can make a difference over time. A lot of your success will depend on how well you can hold your I Positions.

You can also try to find your own peer learning opportunities. I'm going to assume that most people in your position are comfortable using the internet and social media to find groups of people that might be suitable learning groups.

Considerations for advisors to families

If you advise families that are looking at how to best transition their wealth to their rising generation, finding appropriate peer learning opportunities for them can be a great way to stand out as a top resource for them. Even if it isn't a whole peer network, sometimes simply introducing a couple of clients who have similar issues can be the beginning of a win-win-win relationship between your clients and you.

Interdependent Wealth

Interdependent Wealth

CHAPTER 11. PERPETUATION

Whenever people discuss family wealth, the unspoken assumption is that there is a desire for the wealth to last forever. Sometimes it isn't simply a desire for it to last forever; there can be the expectation that it actually will, and much of the planning process is aimed at making that happen.

Depending on the jurisdiction, there may be ways to structure trusts that preserve assets for generations of descendants who are not yet born. This chapter deals with the subject of perpetuation and the fact that we often try to look so far down the road that we lose touch with reality.

Also, if you have ever seen an image of a tree that includes the root structure, you know that what is below the ground will largely govern what's above the ground. Every large, healthy tree is undoubtedly supported by a strong root structure. In case you haven't figured out where you stand in this metaphor, you are the trunk of the tree. The roots are your ancestors, and the branches are your descendants. We'll play with that metaphor a bit later in this chapter.

Systems Thinking and the Time Factor

Let's do some systems thinking again, but this time we will add a new element: time. (Please forgive the unscientific nature of the discussion that follows. I am not a scientist; I don't even play one on TV.)

When a system is in equilibrium, there are a bunch of relationships that are relatively stable. People have found ways to relate to each other that work, even if some people are less than satisfied and others are very happy.

Over time, things can and do change, however. A couple of chapters ago we talked about an emerging champion stating and maintaining an I-Position towards the others in the system. This is one of the ways the system changes as the members of the system adapt to the new realities of one of its members.

There are, of course, other key ways that system equilibrium is affected over time. Membership in the system is fluid by the very nature of the fact that people come and go. Whenever someone is born into a family, the system changes. That person is probably a couple of decades away from having any direct effect on family dynamics, but as soon as they arrive, the system is composed differently than before.

People also leave the system via death. While it is true that some people continue to cast a large shadow even from the grave, when people die, the system is forever changed.

People enter and exit family systems in other ways as well, notably through marriage and other forms of couple hood and through divorce.

Short Term versus Long Term, Backward versus Forward

In the short term, a system will remain at equilibrium, to the point where some people will complain of stagnation and think things will never change. In the longer term, every family system can expect arrivals and departures to change the system markedly, in addition to changes that come from individual members adjusting how they relate to the system.

My view is that the best person to help us look at the right timing for studying a system is Goldilocks.

Most people probably spend too much time worrying about the insignificant day-to-day details of their lives, which, in the end, really don't make that big a difference. Meanwhile, many people also focus way too much energy on things that are so far down the road that it is impossible to have much control on the eventual outcome. I prefer to think about and plan for the parts that are in between, sort of what Goldilocks would choose to concentrate on. When you think about it, that still leaves a heck of a big timeframe to contend with.

In the world of Bowen Family Systems Theory, a certain amount of focus is placed put on creating your family diagram, going back as many generations as you can. One of the main goals of this exercise is to learn as much as possible about who you are and why you are the way you are. The premise is that those who came before you, and the way they were and the things they experienced, are all part of you.

I have witnessed some interesting presentations by people who showed their family diagrams and recounted fascinating stories about what various ancestors lived through, and the stories are typically compelling. It is not a stretch to say that many parts of those stories just make so much more sense when told with the accompanying diagram than they would if the same information were relayed with words only.

And I am not talking here about people telling stories about their families for the purpose of entertaining a room full of people. The stories have to do with the peer learning we were talking about earlier. When a Bowen follower puts their family diagram on the screen or the board and begins to relate a story about their family members to other Bowen people, there is usually a feeling of anticipation, if only because we know that something with an "ah-ha" feeling to it will likely come out in the story, such as repeating patterns from previous generations.

So many aspects of people's lives make so much more sense when they are viewed in the context of where the person was in the family and what the circumstances were in their family or

Interdependent Wealth

origin. In turn, that family of origin and its circumstances were strongly influenced by the families of origin of the two parents who began the new family.

See Figures 11.1 & 11.2

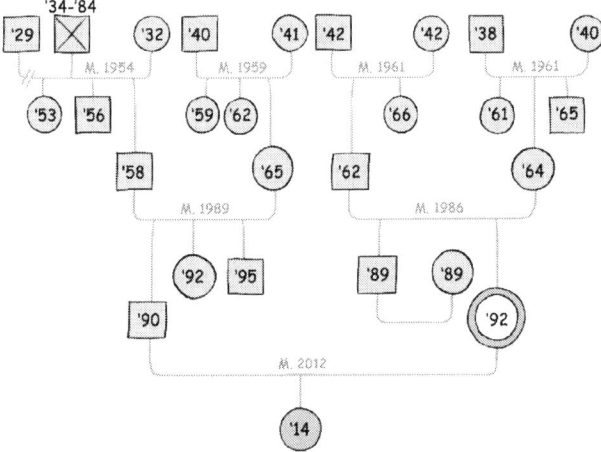

Figures 11.1

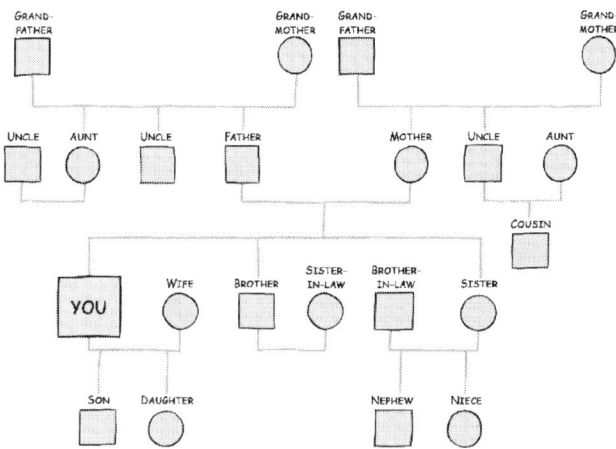

Figure 11.2

How Far Back, How Far Forward?

Some Bowen trainees and faculty can go back to great-great grandparents because they have put in a lot of effort and are highly interested in the subject. Today's technology and websites on ancestry certainly make this easier. But most people go back only to their own grandparents and probably not much further, at least not with much confidence in the details.

If you know all four of your grandparents' names you are probably doing better than average. Some Bowen people will implore you to go back and investigate and get as much information as you can, and I get that. If you are interested and motivated, by all means do it. But I'm going to borrow from the tree roots and branches analogy I used earlier to make what I think is an important point. It also fits with the appropriate timeline that I suggest families focus on.

Yes, going back to the time before your grandparents can yield some interesting facts that may be nice to know and potentially enlightening. And yes, planning to make sure that some assets are preserved for your great-grandchildren may sound like a laudable goal. But rather than worry about how to prepare some assets for some people I will probably never meet, I'd prefer to focus on preparing my own children for whatever assets they will be getting from me.

I think that when we look back to our parents and grandparents, we capture most of what is salient in the lives we are living today. Likewise, if we look at our children and then their (eventual) children, that's about as far as anyone can hope to readily influence. That's five generations, and that's probably enough.

Unexpected Changes and the 100-Year Plan

We've already mentioned system entries and exits, which can greatly change what we hope will happen. We haven't even touched on the fact that the business and the wealth the family own are subject to all sorts of changes resulting from technology, product life cycles, business risk and whatever other market realities you haven't anticipated.

Some of the leaders in the field of "purposeful planning" – which I fully support – have some strong views that families should have a "100-year outlook" or plan for their business. From the first time I read about this, I was shaking my head, thinking that this is simply a bridge too far for most families to even fathom. As I learned that more and more people were getting on this bandwagon and talking about it, I slowly started to warm up to the idea. I mean, what's wrong with looking really far down the road?

But while I have tried to support that line of thinking, it still never sat well with me, and I'll tell you why. I just think that after looking down two generations (to your grandchildren) or, say, 50 years, anything else is just pie in the sky guessing and hoping.

If you really want to look forward more than two generations, then draw your family diagram and try to fill in the facts from more than two generations of your ancestors, because those facts may enlighten you. Nobody can look 100 years into the future. Look back 100 years and consider your ancestors in 1919. How many of them could have conceived even a fraction of what the world is like today? So because we have no idea how lives will be lived or what families will look like 100 years from now, we really can't plan that far in advance.

Human Capital – One Generation at a Time

Back near the beginning of this book, I talked about the time when "my wealth" becomes "our wealth." The key thing that I tell families to work on is to make sure the next generation of leaders is prepared for the wealth they will be inheriting. What that means is making sure the human capital is the focus of the work and the planning.

Are the members of the rising generation capable of managing what they will be expected to manage, and to work together to make the decisions and solve the problems they will be confronted with?

Sure, it makes sense to look at structures and methods to save on taxes that will be owed as the current generation exits the system; those types of tactics are certainly worth exploring. But the overall strategy employed to perpetuate a family's wealth must be centered on the people and on finding ways to increase the odds that they will be able to maintain and build the family wealth together.

Considerations for families

A family looking to keep their hard-earned wealth in the hands of the family has many options. Their advisors will likely be specialists in certain tactics that have been useful to others and could also be beneficial to their family, too.

Before travelling too far down any of those tactical roads, it behooves every family to first look at the people to whom this wealth is being transitioned and to co-create a strategy with them that will work, considering the human capital they represent. Once the strategy has been created, then and only then should the tactical specialists be brought in to properly put all the pieces together.

Considerations for motivated individuals in the family

As the motivated person who sees the need for the family to begin to work on the elements of a successful wealth transition, one of the biggest obstacles is often the outside advisors mentioned above. When family leaders are not sure what to do, they are often at the mercy of their trusted advisors, who will likely have some very good ideas. When the family leaders hear a good idea from someone they trust, they are apt to go with it, even if they have not fully explored where it fits in the big picture.

Someone needs to remind them to focus on the family first and to make sure the family works out the big-picture plan first, based on what makes sense for that family, before getting the experts to put their tactical plans in place.

Considerations for advisors to families

If you advise families who are looking to transition their wealth, you may feel like some of the previous paragraphs are directed at you. That may be so; it depends on how you present your services to your family clients.

I think that if you have read this far in this book, you likely recognize that what I am saying makes sense, even if you don't necessarily see how you can actually make this happen. I bet you have part of the ideal solution for many of your clients, and I also bet you would love for all your clients to end up with the best possible solution for their needs too.

That may take a team of advisors working together; in fact, it almost surely does. Can you ask your client which other advisors they trust and then work with them?

Interdependent Wealth

Interdependent Wealth

CHAPTER 12. SUBJECTIVITY

Wanting to make something good last as long as possible comes naturally to just about everyone. When you have a family you care about on one hand, and a business and wealth on the other, it is probably a given that you will want to find as many ways as possible to integrate the best of those two parts of your world. When you are the person at the heart of the attempt to do that, a few things can come together that make it more difficult.

Because you are so close to both the family and the business or wealth, you naturally believe you are best placed to be at the centre of everything involved in combining them. And that is when you are possibly too close to the situation to truly be the ideal person to lead the task. When you are too close to any situation, your views can be clouded by that closeness. There is a reason that surgeons don't operate on family members.

In this chapter we're going to look at subjectivity in some of its many forms, especially as it affects family wealth transitions.

Independent Directors and Objectivity

Let's begin with a business system example. Once a family business survives its first couple of decades, it is usually important to formalize the governance of the business by creating a board of directors. Many founders put this off as long as possible because they prefer to run everything by the seat of their proverbial pants, like they always have. My dad used to jokingly talk about the board meeting he had held that morning – in the shower. Our business never got to the stage I am talking about here, but had we not sold when we did, it surely would have been a next step.

What happens in many family businesses that are encouraged to set up a board of directors is that they simply name members of the family to the board positions. "There, we have our board," is the feeling. "Now leave us alone."

That's a start and it's probably better than nothing, but surely insufficient in the long run. Eventually, someone important (like a banker or lawyer) will point out that a "real" board will also include some people from outside the family. At this point it is tempting to add some folks who are friendly and therefore easy to control. That's barely better than having only family members, but at least it's a move in the right direction.

Major steps forward occur when truly independent outsiders are put on the board, and then when the outsiders eventually become the majority.

All of that can take decades, but that isn't necessarily a bad thing. I always prefer to look for progress instead of perfection. Slow changes that give everyone time to adjust are better than quick changes that shock the system. It is important to retain some stability and equilibrium.

One of the biggest elements that these non-family outsiders bring with them, aside from their experience, is their objectivity. The family leaders who are in a position to evaluate their own family members are often in a really poor position to do so properly. The tendency to either severely over-estimate or under-estimate one's family members is just so prevalent.

If you've ever been involved in children's sports you have surely seen parents who coach a team and treat their own children in ways that are way out of line with the abilities everyone else clearly sees. And there are examples on both extremes, from the coach who treats their talented child too harshly, to the middling performer that the parent-coach always puts out there in key situations. When you are too close to a person and a situation, it is really difficult to remain fully objective, even when you know you need to.

Professional Trustees

The world of trusts, a topic in which I don't have as much hands-on knowledge, is another area where the issue of subjectivity can rear its ugly head. When assets are held in trusts for people, the process of appointing appropriate trustees is often not given proper attention.

This lack of attention can be because it seems like a small detail when the trust is being set up, because it feels like any decisions are far in the future, or because of a desire to keep things "in the family." But many trusts are set up with what I will call suboptimal trustees.

I'm not a huge fan of the restrictions involved in trusts or the way that beneficiaries are often treated as entitled brats, but having the right trustees – objective and independent – can go a long way towards improving the effectiveness of a trust.

Business Ownership vs. Management

Another subject I would feel remiss if I did not mention is the difference between managing a family business and owning the business.

A large percentage of the family businesses that have become household names are companies that the founding family now simply owns as a strategic asset. There aren't likely many Waltons working at Wal-Mart or Fords working at Ford. These business families have "graduated" to the point where they own or partially own the business, perhaps sit on the board and hire the best people to run it for them. When you think about it, what is the likelihood that the best person to run a business is also someone related to the founder? Not very high.

In smaller family businesses, and those that have not been around long enough to reach that stage, one of the things that constantly causes problems is family members who work in the business. It might be the perception that some family members are overpaid or not doing a good job, it might be that they seem to be taking advantage of others who don't work in the business, or it could simply be that they are not very transparent about business decisions and how they are being made.

Certainly, some highly subjective – that is, emotion-based – questions come up when some family members work for or lead a business, in contrast to situations where the family has only an ownership role.

Bowen on Subjectivity

One of Murray Bowen's areas of focus was the differences between feeling and thinking. He contrasted the emotional system and the feelings that come with it with the intellectual system, better characterized by thinking.

He carried that distinction further, into the realms of subjectivity and objectivity. My shorthand version is as follows:

Emotional: Feeling = Subjective

Intellectual: Thinking = Objective

This is a gross oversimplification of Bowen's work in these areas, but for the purposes of this chapter I'm going to go with it. But I should again note that this is my own understanding of this concept.

My Own Bowen Project: An Overly Subjective Relationship

So far we have looked at a few areas in which the ideas of objectivity and subjectivity can affect family wealth transitions. But the real heart of this chapter is a formative experience that I had early in my Bowen training.

Let me set the stage and remind you of some of the Bowen training basics I have discovered. Recall that learning Bowen Family Systems Theory is not something you can necessarily do simply by reading about it. You could read every book ever written about swimming, but if you've never been in the water, I doubt you will ever feel like you've really learned about it.

Having said that, when people start dipping their toes in the Bowen pool, they usually prefer to stay in the shallow end. But as I have told many people who have inquired about my Bowen path, I'm not sure there even is a shallow end in the Bowen pool.

I have to credit my Bowen coach, who happened to be the person who ran the program in Vermont where I started this journey. He was the coach of my small group in the afternoon portion of the monthly program, where I took turns with the others presenting some personal family issue or scenario. My coach and I also met for coaching sessions via Skype once a month to talk about whatever subject was on my mind.

During the second year of my involvement in the training program, my coach was getting to know me pretty well, and while he didn't like to be too directive in his approach, which I appreciated, he did keep coming back to the same issue, month after month.

Although it was phrased in a way that was not strictly an "order" – "you need to do this" – he was persistent enough to nudge me into what was effectively the deep end of the Bowen pool. His words varied a bit from time to time, but usually included the fact that he thought my relationship with my father was too subjective. Sometimes he switched it up and noted that my relationship with Dad could stand to be "more objective."

I tried to ignore him the first few times, thinking he must not have been paying close attention when I spoke to him or that he was ignoring an important fact on the family diagram I drew. There was clearly an X drawn through the square that represented my father, since he had been dead for over five years. How the heck was I supposed to work on my relationship with him?

Well, of course Murray Bowen had an answer for that.

So we looked at my family diagram and my coach asked me some questions about some of the shapes near the top that did not have X's drawn through them. "What about your aunt, or your uncle?" True, my dad's older sister and younger brother were still around, but what do they have to do with this?

After much encouragement, there I was at my aunt's house, sitting at the kitchen table, asking her questions about her family of origin. My uncle was also there, thankfully, to help clarify some of the details. My aunt was so excited that someone was interested in this subject that she was talking a mile a minute and switching back and forth between English and the German dialect our family used.

We soon got over the splashing and flailing phase of my jumping into the pool. I quickly learned to tread water and started to enjoy it. We spent a few hours together, with me asking a few basic questions about what it was like growing up in the home with my dad as her little brother, and the stories were very enlightening.

I was suddenly picturing my dad in a whole new way. When the discussion came to their move to Canada and the circumstances around that, I had a whole new appreciation for everything the family had gone through to get to where we were today.

I can tell you that when I reported back to my coach afterwards, smiling from ear to ear about the experience, he looked back at me with what seemed like an "I told you so" smile.

Of course while part of me felt like I was now off the hook, having done my homework, that didn't last very long. He let me bask in the glow for a bit and then asked what was next on my journey of discovery through my family diagram.

It dawned on me that I had lots of questions for my mother that I had never asked, and so I was able to follow up with her on a long drive we took together. Boy, did I learn a few stories that cast so many things in a new light.

From Subjective to Objective

I will now try to explain the whole idea of going from a subjective to an objective relationship, from my experience, my understanding of Bowen Theory and my own point of view. I should note that I did two presentations of this project to Bowen audiences soon afterwards and nobody told me that I was dead wrong. Nobody came and asked for my autograph either, I should add.

The way I explained it in those presentations was that I had struggled with the idea of what a subjective relationship was and with how to make it more objective. Bowen recommended that trainees work on their adult-to-adult relationships with as many living members on their family diagram as possible, because that is the best path to increasing one's differentiation of self. By deepening my relationship with my aunt, and to some extent my uncle too, I was able to add their perspectives to my views of my father.

Previously, the views I held of my dad were mine and mine alone. They were subjective because they were based on my own feelings. Many of those feelings included some perceptions of things that were not exactly factual. By asking for and receiving new information from others who knew him from way back, from his formative days in his own family of origin, I was able to add new perspectives to the viewpoints I had held before.

When I added new information and other views to my own perspective, my relationship was able to go from quite subjective to more objective. It also felt like I was now able to set down a heavy backpack that I had been unwittingly walking around with for decades, and that was a big step forward for me.

That's my story and I'm sticking to it.

Since then, I have continued to mull over this subject and have expanded my thinking on it. I now like to add the systems view into the mix as well.

Recall the idea of a system being a bunch of dots with lines connecting them. Now take yourself out of the system and look at it from above to try to get a more objective look at how the dots fit together. You can draw some of the lines thicker based on stronger relationships and others thin because relationships are weaker.

My original view of my relationship with my father was along one of the thick lines, and by adding some new information from some of the other connections, I was seeing a truer picture of reality, one that was more objective and less subjective.

Considerations for families

If you don't yet have any neutral third parties (from outside the family) involved as board members or advisors, what are you waiting for? Please recognize that you are not likely going to be able to do everything by yourself. It isn't because you don't know enough or aren't close enough to your family, it is because you are too close.

Considerations for motivated individuals in the family

If you are the person who expects to play the key relationship role in the family wealth transition, you could do worse than to take a page from Murray Bowen's book and work on as many of your adult-to-adult relationships as you can. This process will demand someone who has the objectivity required to make the transition work, even when everyone else is looking at things from their own subjective point of view – especially so in those circumstances.

Considerations for advisors to families

If you have client families in which the person you work with "knows" there are things they should be doing in relation to the wealth transition, but they always seem to have reasons (excuses?) for kicking the can down the road, please continue to raise the issue. And when they tell you they haven't had time and they will get to it, smile at them and say you understand. But then bring it up again next time, maybe more firmly, and maybe with some other ideas or tips or first steps or an introduction to someone who can be a resource for them.

Interdependent Wealth

CHAPTER 13. TOP-HEAVY TRIANGLES

We are now going to enter the world of triangles. The concept of the triangle is a huge part of BFST; it even warrants a place among the famous eight concepts.

Alas, for me it remains something of a head scratcher, as it seems to be for others I have dealt with. I will try to capture the essence of what I think Bowen was getting at when he expounded upon the importance of triangles, while also tying in my own views of the wealth transition process and how triangles might be looked at there.

Triangles as the Basic Building Block

Bowen called the triangle the "basic building block" of the emotional system. He clearly believed this was new and useful to the way we think about systems of people because he included it in his eight concepts.

According to Bowen, any two-person group can be stable as long as things are calm, but as soon as you add any uncertainty or anxiety to the situation, one of the people will search for a third person so they can become more comfortable again. This should not be difficult for anyone to relate to; we have all seen many versions of this, and we see them every day: "Just wait until your father gets home" many mothers have uttered when dealing with a young child. And countless fathers have said, "What does your mother say about it?" Likewise, there are situations where it is the child who cannot wait for the other parent to get home so they can try to ease their discomfort.

Of course triangles do not appear only in parent-child scenarios, they occur among siblings, co-workers, congregations, social groups, classmates, teams and wherever people are involved in groups.

The simplest way I have found to think about triangles is to picture three dots that move around, either closer together or farther apart, depending on whether or not they agree with each other at a given time. As the dots move, the triangle changes shape.

Start with a basic equilateral triangle (three dots all the same distance apart, so the three sides are all the same length). When there is no tension and everyone is in agreement, this is a natural state of equilibrium.

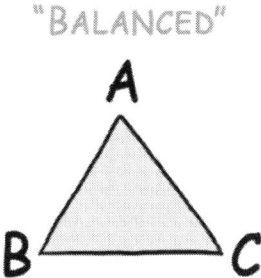

Figure 13.1 Balanced Triangle

As we introduce a contentious issue, two of the dots (people!) have opposing views, which tends to drive them apart. As they distance themselves from each other, they feel a bit lonely and try to draw the third person to their way of thinking so that they can set up a two-against-one.

If A and B are in opposition and trying to woo C, the triangle's shape will change as C moves closer to either A or to B. Let's assume C moves towards B. Now B and C have what is known as the "inside position," while A is on the outside. Picture a long triangle with the B and C dots close together on the left and A much farther away on the right.

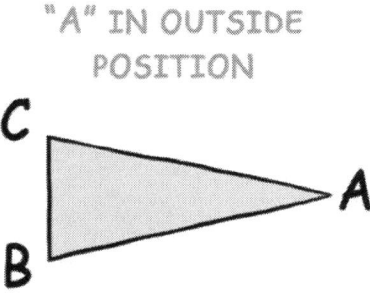

Figure 13.2 "A" in Outside Position

At various points in their discussion, A may work to bring C closer to A's side, and if A is successful, B will be in the outside position, with A and C on the inside.

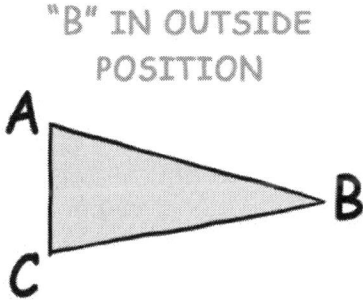

Figure 13.3 "B" in Outside Position

Eventually C may do something that brings A and B closer together, and C can be thrust outside. And of course when any one of them feels the need to reach out to a fourth person, we get into the wonderful world of interlocking triangles.

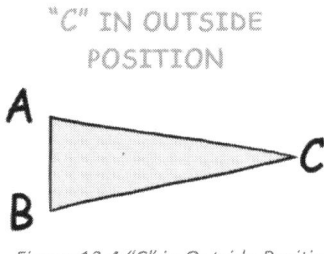

Figure 13.4 "C" in Outside Position

Interlocking Triangles: Simplifying the Complex

A triangle is a more stable unit in the same way that a three-legged stool is more stable than a two-legged one. But most groups consist of more than three people, right? Of course, and that is where the interlocking triangles concept comes in.

Bowen pointed out that any group of people larger than three can be broken down into a series of interlocking triangles. For example, a group of four consists of four interlocking triangles, one comprising each possible group of three people. With five people, there are nine interlocking triangles. As you add people, the number of possible triangles goes up very quickly, and I have no interest in turning this into a math book, so we'll stop here.

I will assume that some of you are waiting for the punch line, as in, okay, I get that three people are a triangle, but so what?

My best understanding of what Bowen was really driving at comes down to the fact that he was a scientist and that he always put his emphasis on observation. To make Bowen Theory into a real science, he needed to be able to observe certain phenomena on a consistent, repeatable basis.

When he had families that included members with schizophrenia come and live in the ward at the hospital, he needed to continue to implore his students and co-researchers to always note what they observed factually. Trying to observe how tension moves around the entire system in a large group of people can seem like an overwhelming task. It was beyond the ability of most of the people who were working with him on this huge project.

Using the idea of triangles, and interlocking triangles, allowed him to make the groups small enough that his people could properly observe behaviours and note those observations consistently. That is what I believe the essence of the triangle came down to as Bowen tried to make progress with his research.

So while the first thing you need to understand about triangles is that they are based on the fact that an uncomfortable person in a two-person system will search for a third party to take their side, the other key feature is that you can use triangles to help break down a complex group of people into more manageable and observable units. When you are working with a multigenerational family in a family meeting that is supposed to provide everyone with a better understanding of what is and what will be, there can often be plenty of tension in the room.

If you are an outsider brought in to guide the process, the sheer number of players can be overwhelming. Using the idea of interlocking triangles can be useful as you observe what is going on and try to make sense of it.

People are often on different sides of key issues. As the discussion proceeds and the anxiety starts to rise, it can be interesting to observe the way people formulate their arguments, trying to sway other key people to their way of thinking. These observations help the facilitator understand the system, thereby allowing them to better guide useful discussions.

The Primary Triangle and Unresolved Emotional Attachment

Let's back up to some of the basics relating to triangles in families. Each person becomes part of their most basic triangle as soon as they are born – that triangle consists of each person and their two parents, the "primary triangle" for the child. This is your family of origin, baby.

This primary triangle and this family of origin will be the source of the most important influences of your life. Likewise, each of your parents was born into a primary triangle with their parents as part of their family of origin, and these were very influential in how they turned out as adults. As you can imagine, or perhaps know from experience, those moments when a little bundle of joy joins the family can be filled with all sorts of emotions.

Each person is born at a unique moment in the development of a family, and the other events occurring simultaneously with that arrival will also have a marked effect on how things develop for the child and on the parents' emotional attachment to the child.

A person's primary triangle will likely be the key triangle of their entire life. In many ways, they will spend the rest of their lives trying to continue to move away from their early parental influences, with varying degrees of success. Bowen himself makes lots of references to "unresolved emotional attachment" to one's parents. It's as if life is just a constant struggle to "resolve" what we were born into and what took place during the early years of our lives.

The entire concept of differentiation of self, when you think about it, has an unwritten question embedded in it. You may have been wondering, "Just who am I trying to differentiate myself from?" Voilà: the answer is (mostly) your parents. When you think about sibling rivalry, how much of it is likely based on how each of the siblings is trying to impress the parents or win their favour, in comparison to their siblings?

Top-Heavy Triangles

The idea of "top-heavy" triangles is one I came up with myself in an attempt to illustrate an idea that seems to cause problems with wealth transitions in many families. This phenomenon most often takes place in families in which the wealth creator – the G1 patriarch – remains a central, and often controlling, figure. (I say patriarch knowing full well there are cases where matriarchs play this role, but an overwhelming majority in history, so far, have been men.)

The "top-heavy" aspect I am ascribing to these leaders has to do with their tendency to dominate just about every aspect of life, be it in the business circle or the family circle. So much attention is paid to these figures that they are often seen as "larger than life" and are treated as such. Situations that include such a figure can be some of the most problematic for families and their advisors to handle.

In each triangle they are part of, these figures usually have a very strong emotional influence because of their stature and position. Everyone wants to please them, and they are often revered by those who work for them. Much of what they do succeeds in bringing people to the inside position of the triangle. At the same time, though, nobody ever feels as if they are truly close to them, because they are so unapproachable.

In triangles with family members, there can be a tendency to want to please this person and therefore side with them even when it may not be in one's best long-term interest to do so.

Take-Home Message

My message here is that the triangles that the dominant family leader is part of may need to be looked at a bit differently than most of the other three-person groups. This idea is not found anywhere in Bowen's work, but it is my observation as a fan of BFST who has seen how some people operate by virtue of their position, their success and their desire to always be in control, often well past the point of their control being in the family's best interest.

The I-Position as Antidote

If you choose to go against someone in a family power position like this, it will be doubly important to make sure you are ready to stand firm in your own I-Position.

The power in these kinds of relationships will eventually be rebalanced into a new equilibrium. Sometimes that occurs only after the leader passes away or is incapacitated by a health problem. But hopefully, with a strong family and great advisors, it can happen at an earlier stage.

The presence of the word "interdependence" in the title of this book stems in large part from thinking about this type of leader and the fact that the sooner they realize that they will not live forever and that the success of their wealth transition depends on them and many others, the better for all.

Considerations for families

If yours is not a family in which one person seems to dominate everything, congratulations – you can probably just take what you've learned about triangles and hopefully observe relationships through a new lens.

If you do have a dominant person who creates a challenging emotional environment, I suggest that you exercise plenty of patience and manage your own expectations. Do what you can vis-à-vis this person, and don't forget to continuously work on all of the other relationships that are important to your long-term success. The more other people you can work with (and work on) to look at the transition situation realistically, the better your chances will be.

Considerations for motivated individuals in the family

If you are faced with a challenging situation with a family leader, I encourage you to focus on being patient and realistic about what is possible. Think about your own I-Positions and work on every other relationship to make sure they are all as strong as can be.

Considerations for advisors to families

Hopefully this basic understanding of triangles will be useful as a new lens through which to look at family relationships. If you have family clients with the over-dominance trait, you know the type I am talking about.

I encourage you to forge relationships with family members other than the leader you normally deal with. That person will not live forever, and if they are your only point of contact, the fact is you will be seen as one of "Dad's guys" and other family members will forget you very quickly after the funeral if you don't build strong relationships with them ahead of time.

If you do get to know other family members, you can become an ally to them as someone who just might have a better chance of getting through to that dominant patriarch or matriarch.

CHAPTER 14. THE IMPORTANCE OF UNSTRUCTURED PLAY TIME

The concept of triangles may be fascinating to some, but it is important to recall that their main purpose, as far as Murray Bowen was concerned, is to help us to observe what is taking place in an emotional system.

Very few human systems are limited to three people, and nowhere in the discussion of triangles is it ever suggested that three people is a magic number for anything other than observation and analysis. In the real world, people get together and are organized into systems ranging from pairs, to handfuls, to dozens, to hundreds.

As the number of people in a system grows, the number of possible triangles grows even larger, so in some ways the idea of looking at triangles doesn't seem to make things any simpler. That's because triangles are meant to clarify what is happening on a micro basis (i.e., within the small group) and not necessarily on a macro basis (within the entirety of the system).

Transfer versus Transition

When we think about multigenerational wealth transitions, we can observe a similar phenomenon, one that has become somewhat of a pet peeve of mine.

The mainstream media and the popular press love to write about a huge wealth transfer that will occur in the coming decade or so as baby boomers age and die. On a macro level, it is true that this will be a "wealth transfer," but the word "transfer" has a tendency to get used again when looking at families on a micro level. But when considering how a family will move their wealth from one generation to the next, "transfer" is simply the wrong way to look at it.

Every family should instead be looking for the best way to transition their wealth, not simply transfer it.

Any family going through such a transition probably could not care less about the macro wealth transition going on in society; they care only about their own family's version. And for the family it is important to look at it as a gradual transition of the wealth, rather than a transfer, which can imply that it all happens in one shot, like transferring money from one account to another, or someone getting transferred at work, where they finish on Friday in one place and start somewhere else on Monday.

The Goldilocks Group

So we now know the triangle is likely too small a group to be truly useful in trying to make sense of an entire family faced with the task of transitioning their wealth down through successive generations. We are also aware that because we read plenty of stories about wealth transfer in society, we may think about the subject from too high a perch – few families care about how the issue affects society – a very large group – since they have their own house to put in order.

So if one group is too small and another is too big, it behooves us to try to figure out which group is just right.
There really never is a one-size-fits-all answer to this question, though, because families and their circumstances are different. Additionally, circumstances change over time, so the "right" answer for a family today may no longer be ideal in a couple of years or even a couple of months.

But the fact that there is no one right answer for any family about the size of the group they should be thinking about doesn't mean we shouldn't talk about types of interactions that families have and about the clues they can offer about how we might want to proceed.

I will once again try to combine ideas from the world of wealth transitions with elements of Bowen Family Systems Theory. Let's start with the field of wealth transitions.

More Is Better Than Fewer

If I could point out one glaring problem based on my experience with and study of the world of intergenerational wealth transitions, it is that the group of people typically involved in its planning, decision-making and execution is usually too small. Too many families still rely on one leader, often the wealth creator, and perhaps that person's spouse to a certain extent, along with outside subject matter experts.

The person who leads the family business or manages the wealth – let's call them "Dad" for simplicity's sake – will talk to the lawyer and the accountant and come up with some ways to take care of some of the pressing issues involved in wealth transition. Hopefully the lawyer and accountant will bring in others to craft a plan that makes sense on many dimensions so that the wealth will be transitioned while minimizing the amount of tax owing and ensuring that everyone will be treated equally.

So far so good, right?

Not really. Any serious plans you have made but have not shared at least with those who will be directly affected by them may be a recipe for disaster.

Am I overstating the case here? Maybe a bit, but there are enough examples of disasters from this type of planning that it would be irresponsible of me not to warn you. Note, too, the phrase I just used: people "directly affected by" the planning. This brings up another important distinction I need to make.

Family Council versus Family Assembly

I have intentionally not ventured too deeply into the area of family governance in this book, but that isn't because I am not a fan of it or not well versed in it. It is simply beyond the scope of what I am trying to do here. But we are talking about groups of people and their potential involvement in wealth transition, so it is now appropriate for some discussion of governance.

A **family council** is typically a group of family members who are chosen to represent all family members on matters that require decision-making on behalf of the overall family. The number of people on a family council generally ranges from 5 to 12, and a council typically has representatives from various family branches and at least two generations. It is a select group, the membership of which is decided by the family and the composition of which is determined by rules that evolve from within the group over time.

A **family assembly** is a much larger group and includes pretty well everyone directly related to the family that you would invite to any major family function, such as a family reunion. It is the largest group of family stakeholders you might imagine. They are stakeholders insofar as they are interested in the family and its business and wealth, because it affects them in some way, even if only indirectly.

Note that I am casting the largest net possible in my definition, and that I fully realize that families will rightfully look at the list of people who would be included in my definition and exclude some as not really belonging. If you have ever been involved in trying to decide who gets invited to a wedding and who doesn't, you are surely familiar with this type of exercise and how much "fun" it can be.

Bowen and the Family Retreat

Families that have successfully transitioned their wealth for several generations have almost always incorporated some form of family retreat into their routine. A family assembly is typically the group that would be invited to a family retreat. Family retreats are often held every one, two or three years and typically involve a large number of guests. Retreats are usually a few days long, or even up to a week. Some part of that time is devoted to sharing updates on the family's business; much of the event is designed to encourage connections between people who are related but who perhaps don't know each other very well.

Everyone who seriously advises wealthy families always talks about the importance of family meetings, and they are very important, but we need to broaden the advice to include various kinds of meetings.

Most of the family meeting advice is directed at the smaller family group, usually just the parents and adult children, and that is of course an important step that shouldn't be overlooked, especially as wealth transition plans are being created. But eventually, as the family grows and those meetings become too unwieldy for decision-making, a family council will be useful. These smaller family meetings are key to moving the wealth discussions out of the "too-small" group of Dad and his lawyer.

But the area where Bowen Family Systems Theory most closely connects with the notion of the family assembly and family retreats is the concept of, well, connection.

Adult-to-Adult Resourcefulness

Recall my story a few chapters ago about meeting with my aunt to talk about her family of origin, which included my father. Ideally, that type of meeting wouldn't have to be set up as a special occasion, it would occur in a more random and matter-of-fact fashion.

A big part of the whole idea of differentiation of self is predicated on the fact that you know the other people in your extended family, as individuals, thanks to real face-to-face contact with them. This isn't so much about knowing all the details of each person's life as it is about being on good terms with people and knowing and caring enough about them to have some meaningful connection.

There is already some familial connection, on paper, on the family diagram. But so often, that's all there is, to the point where just reaching out to someone can feel weird. When you work on these relationships, even just casually, but regularly, these connections get much smoother.

Believe me, I am not saying this stuff is always easy to do, because it isn't, especially when it has been ignored or non-existent for years or decades. What I am saying is that a bit of effort and persistence, combined with the right attitude and some curiosity, can go a long way to ameliorating family relationships.

The goal is adult-to-adult relationships built not on helping anyone or asking anyone to help you, but just on a connection. The more connections you have with extended family members, the more potential resources you have in your family system. One of the saddest things that can happen is when a family member could use a resource, and they don't know there is someone in their extended family who could provide it. A resource can be as simple as someone you can ask a question, get a referral from or bounce an idea off of.

Activities for Family Retreats and Family Councils

When families plan retreats to share information about the family's business, there can be a temptation to over-structure the time spent together and to focus too much on sharing the financial and business information, to the detriment of social interaction and downtime.

I've seen various suggestions to avoid this situation, including breaking the time up into business, education and fun activities. One of the often overlooked items to plan for is... unplanned time. When family members have a chance to just hang out together it is amazing how their bonds can be strengthened by simple virtue of experiencing the time together as members of the same tribe.

The same general thoughts extend to smaller family groups that need to convene regularly for decision-making, such as a family council. If all the meetings are business heavy and little time is spent on less urgent matters, it can be a huge missed opportunity. Of course everyone is busy, with work and their own nuclear families, but if the members of those groups do not spend enough fun time or social time together, you can bet that meetings will not run as smoothly as they would if everyone had the chance to know each other better and more objectively.

The meaningful connections that can develop without the need for a formal agenda are key. Families that play together as well as work together do better together. When family members get the chance to experience things together and grow together, those interactions add up to the creation of groups of people who learn how to function well together, for the good of the whole family.

Considerations for families

If your family is all business, all the time, that will probably start to catch up to you sooner or later. Look for ways to increase the number of occasions when people gather and don't just talk business. Also, there are probably family members from inside the business who would do well to work on bettering their relationships with those outside the business.
This work cannot start too soon. If you think I'm talking to you, then you're probably right.

Considerations for motivated individuals in the family

If you are the one who sees that your family is too much of an all-business family and that there should be more interaction that's not business related, speak up. Get others on board and start planning and organizing non-business get-togethers. Plan something small and go from there. Don't expect everyone to buy in and be gung-ho at the outset, but just keep making progress and win them over one event and one person at a time.

Considerations for advisors to families

I've been suggesting that advisors do whatever they can to get to know their family clients better. If you have big family clients and you don't know their children yet, maybe you can provide a win-win opportunity.

Are you in a position to offer an experience to your best client families that will allow you to get to know their kids, and at the same time provide the family with a more social event? If so, what are you waiting for?

CHAPTER 15. SIMPLE VERSUS EASY

As I write this in November 2018, my hope is that in both the near and distant future, readers will feel something similar to what I am going through right now.

Writing this book has been a fun challenge for me. Hopefully for readers it has also been fun. Writing a book is a great example of the difference between two words that get mixed up far too often – simple and easy.

Writing a book is simple. It is not easy. Family wealth transition is like that.

The Answers Are Not in the Book

Now that we are near the end of the book, I can confess something I would not have stated up front. The answers to your family wealth transition problems are not in this book. I trust that while you may find that a bit strange at first glance, upon further reflection you will understand what I am driving at. A lot of books are written by experts who are really good at certain things, so much so that they truly believe what they do is easily replicable by just about anyone who takes the time to read their book and apply the new knowledge. If only!

Other books are written by people who have met some challenging obstacles in life, and they too think that because they were able to find a way to overcome their obstacles, with this newfound knowledge you too will be able to surmount your challenges and succeed. I have read plenty of books in my life that fall into these categories.

I hope you haven't found this book to be either type. At times, you may have felt I was trying to make the work of transitioning family wealth seem easy. I apologize for that, because I know that where the rubber meets the road, in those key family discussions that need to happen, most of what I have written about here can be really difficult. It is not easy, at least not for most people.

But some families have succeeded, and thankfully for all of us, an industry of sorts has come into being in the past few decades and the stories of how those families have succeeded are being shared more and more. Not only are the stories being learned, but researchers and practitioners have been working hard to extract the most important common elements of those stories and to make those lessons available to other families.

The goal of those people, and my own goal in many respects, is to clarify what the most important considerations are when a family faces choices and decisions regarding the way they plan for their wealth and how it will move to their rising generation. At least seeing what works for some families, or better still, many families, can give you a sort of roadmap that you can try to emulate, while at the same time recognizing that your family will need its own custom variation of what worked elsewhere.

Sometimes just knowing that something is possible can be a great catalyst, especially when you can adopt some of the key elements that contributed to making it work. Having some clarity about what needs to happen can help to simplify what lies ahead, but again, that doesn't imply that doing it in your own family will be easy.

What to Do versus How to Do It

Even when you do have a better idea of what other families have done, you rarely have much detail on how they went about it. This fact highlights the folly of those who bring in outsiders and ask them what they should do. Those experts are apt to recycle what they did for some other family, on the assumption that your family will benefit exactly as the other family did.

But my contention is that you already know what you need to do; you just may need lots of help with how you should go about getting it done. The what is transitioning the wealth to the next generation in a way that maintains family harmony and gives the wealth the greatest chance of being a positive influence in the lives of all family members.
The devil is in the details of the how.

An Example of How Bowen Illuminates Wealth Transition: "You Are Wrong. Change Back. Or Else!"

Recall that one of my reasons for writing this book was to illustrate some of the ways that Bowen Family Systems Theory can illuminate the work involved in making these wealth transitions successful.

Like wealth transition itself, Bowen Theory is not simple, although I have tried to highlight some of its simpler aspects. My feeling is that BFST, like most subjects, does become simpler the more you study it. I have been at it for only a few years, and it is beginning to seem simpler to me. But that still doesn't make it easy.

One of the best illustrations of a part of Bowen Theory that is simple yet not easy is the I-Position that we've spoken about a few times. It sure sounds simple to figure out what you will do and what you will not do. When you need to put it into practice, though, you quickly discover that it is not as easy as you hoped.

In Murray Bowen's attempt to move his theory towards being a science, he concentrated on observing how things happened in the real world to see if he could identify repeatable, predictable patterns of responses. Knowing in advance what is likely to

happen can make the simple things you are trying to accomplish a bit easier. So here is the final BFST tidbit that I will share.
As you make a stand and share a new I-Position with members of your family, you can expect them to react to this potential disruption to the existing equilibrium. Your disruption will be met, according to Bowen, with a predictable, three-stage response:

1. You are wrong.
2. Change back.
3. If you do not, here are the consequences.

You already knew that taking a stand with your family would not necessarily be met with warm, understanding acceptance. But when you are able to summon some knowledge of Bowen Theory in your mind in advance, it is definitely a bit easier. You can almost turn it into a curious pursuit, as you see how closely your family's reaction will come to Bowen's prediction:

"Hey, he was right – they are telling me everything that's wrong with my new stance. So far so good... Hmm, now they're strongly suggesting (insisting?) that I change back! Wow, pretty much as expected... Oh, here comes the consequences part. But they are still being vague about what they will do if I continue holding firm."

Give it a chance. Maybe ask them what the consequences will be.

"Oh, wow, that didn't take long." Looks like Bowen Theory is actually pretty useful.

But just because knowledge of the theory can make some things a bit easier, it still doesn't make them easy! Bowen is not simple, and it has never felt particularly accessible to most people I have spoken to about it. If you were hoping to read this book and then be able to say that you now understand Bowen

Theory, I think you will be at least slightly underwhelmed. As I said above, the answers are not in this book.

If, however, you are from a family with a wealth transition on the horizon, or you advise such families, I think I have shown you a number of ways that BFST does illuminate how families can be more successful as they face that task.

If you have been inspired to go out and search for more information and learning so that you too can be better trained in BFST, especially if it is so you can be even better at working with family wealth transitions, then I thank you in advance for those endeavours. I don't think you will regret it. Just don't expect the work to be easy.

Then again, if you are already working in this field, you know there isn't a lot that's easy. Most of it isn't even simple!

Considerations for families

If you are a family facing an upcoming wealth or business transition from one generation to the next, I encourage you to be more intentional about those efforts.

One of my favourite expressions in this area is "things don't just happen all by themselves." You need to work at things, with intention and diligence and follow-up, if you expect to make progress. When you think about it, that is really no different than what you do in any other important area of your life. You need to make this a priority. It is a lot of work, but it will be well worth it in the end.

The alternative is to wait and do nothing. Families that have tried that approach have typically come to regret their inaction. Every day that you wait, the fewer good options you will have and the fewer chances you will have to correct your course along the way. So please get moving. If you aren't sure where to begin, pick up **SHIFT Your Family Business** for ideas. It's available on Amazon and it was written by one of your favourite authors!

Considerations for motivated individuals in the family

The "motivated individuals" for whom I have been writing these closing notes at the end of each chapter are often the unsung heroes of the family. I want to acknowledge the fact that these people exist in many families and often lurk beneath the surface for years, and even when they do make positive contributions to the family by taking needed action, their input is typically undervalued.

For the few families where the motivated person is also the head of the family and the one most in charge of the wealth, your chances of success are obviously the greatest.

For all of you motivated to be positive contributors to a successful wealth transition, I encourage you to focus on progress instead of perfection. Don't set unreasonable expectations for the family or for yourself. If you can move things along from quarter to quarter or month to month, that will make a difference year over year too.

It is a long road and will appear longest at the outset, but please persevere and work on building a network of other like-minded and like-hearted people in the extended family who will come aboard with you. It will be less lonely and you will make more progress together.

Considerations for advisors to families

For all the people who work in this field as advisors to families, I think you know that many of the families need this and they need someone to point them in the right direction. They need objective outsiders who can see their family members through independent and more objective eyes, and who can keep them on track.

Families also need people they trust to clarify and coordinate all the work that other advisors will be called on to do to make all the planning work. You can make a huge potential value-added difference for your most important clients by being that coordinator.

My wish for you is that you join the Purposeful Planning Institute and become part of the wonderful way the field is progressing.

Interdependent Wealth

PART III. TAKEAWAYS AND NEXT STEPS

Interdependence as the Key

A family is a system, meaning that family members do not simply exist as a list of people with common ancestors, but as a group of people linked together through relationships. When some family members take it upon themselves to act as if they have control over all other family members, on the assumption that that control will last forever, they are fooling themselves. You can control some of the people all of the time, and all of the people some of the time, but you cannot control everyone all of the time, because some of them will outlive you. The sooner the leaders of a family accept that they are only here for a limited time, the better. Eventually, they need to begin to act like that is the reality as well.

As I hope the examples in this book have demonstrated, the key thing about interdependence is that while we really cannot change anyone but ourselves, when we change how we act, others will change as well, because we are part of a system. Bowen Family Systems Theory is an attempt to explain, understand and predict how one person's changes can bring about changes in others.

Thanks to what BFST has taught us, we are in a better position to think about – and act in – ways that increase the likelihood that what we do and say will positively contribute to the changes we are hoping to effect in our family systems.

Future Work and an Invitation

BFST covers a broad scope of human activity and it surely affects family wealth transitions in ways I have not even thought of; I've just provided some examples. Perhaps in the future there will be a platform where interested parties can learn from these ideas and share more examples with each other.

I would like to conclude with an invitation to please get in touch if this book has touched you in any way. I recall years ago, before the internet, my dad had read a book and asked his secretary to track the person down. Somehow she did, and Dad called him up. I was mortified when I heard the story. Why would Dad "bother" this author?

I could not have been more wrong. Now having written a book myself I can tell you that I love to get feedback from readers. And now that the internet does exist (I guess it wasn't just a fad!) it is so easy to connect with people on LinkedIn or Twitter or via email. Here's how you can connect with me:

- **Email:** Steve@FamilyLegacyShift.com.
- **Websites:** www.ShiftYourFamilyBusiness.com and www.InterdependentWealth.com.
- **Twitter:** @FamilyLegacyAdv
- **LinkedIn:** https://www.linkedin.com/in/steve-legler-259065a
- **YouTube:** https://www.youtube.com/channel/UCX26tZkhSZipAWWmASgWbsg or search Steve Legler Family Business and you will find me.

Interdependent Wealth

Interdependent Wealth

APPENDIX

OTHER HUMAN RELATIONSHIP SYSTEMS ORGANIZATIONS

Organization and Relationship Systems Coaching (ORSC)

After studying Bowen Theory for a couple of years, I stumbled upon a great organization devoted to training coaches and facilitators who work with interrelated groups of people. The ORSC has a series of five 3-day workshops, which I have taken, that provide all sorts of exercises and tools that coaches and facilitators can use with groups. The ORSC also offers an extensive coaching certification program for those who have taken the five courses.

It is not family systems work, but I did get a lot out of the ORSC's courses and highly recommend its training for anyone working with groups in facilitation or coaching roles.

Human Systems Dynamics Institute (HSDI)

During my ORSC work, another attendee told me about the HSDI. I have attended a few HSDI webinars and found its tools and techniques quite useful. It also offers in-person training and certification, which I have not taken. I believe the HSDI has a lot to offer those who work with groups.

Coaches Training Institute (CTI)

When I was starting the Family Enterprise Advisor program in 2013, one of my classmates suggested I look into some coaching training. I was skeptical at first, but asked her which of the dozens of coaching programs I should look at. She referred me to CTI, and it turned out to be the best advice I could ever have taken.

CTI offers a series of five introductory workshops, each three days long. I took these courses in 2013–14 and they were instrumental in my career shift from a guy who worked in a family business and family office to a guy who was actually equipped to work with other families.

CTI also offers a certification program to those who have completed the five courses. I chose not to go through the certification at the time because I was not sure I really wanted to be a coach. That will very likely change in the near future.

Interdependent Wealth

Interdependent Wealth

ACKNOWLEDGEMENTS

This book is part of my journey through the world of family business and family wealth. The journey began in my family of origin over five decades ago and has also included my wife's family for the past quarter century plus. Our own nuclear family began in 1999 and eventually that will become more of the focus of our transitions.

But it has been only a handful of years since I felt called to serve other families to which I am not related, and that work has been very rewarding and a great learning experience. I am very grateful for the select families that have welcomed me into their circle

I also want to acknowledge the people who read my blogs and newsletters, watch my videos and engage with me on social media. I cannot tell you how rewarding it is to learn that the things I am sharing are useful to others, especially those who are working to improve the field of helping families overcome the challenges of wealth transition.

I need to thank Judi Cunningham for creating the Family Enterprise Advisor program. There is no better education program for people in this field and I was lucky enough to stumble upon it so close to home. A few other instructors I met there that I continue to exchange with at conferences are David Bentall, Wendy Sage-Hayward and Ruth Steverlynck. Thanks to all four for inspiring me and continuing to encourage my work in this space.

From the Bowen world, the faculty at the Bowen Center are too numerous to mention individually, but their efforts have been instrumental in my appreciation for, and learning of, all things Bowen. Particular thanks go to my BFST coach, Amie Post, who was never afraid to push me harder than I wanted to be pushed. I was always mentally drained after our many exchanges, but it was always a good kind of tired.

Also from the Bowen world, I'm happy to be part of the online Bowen Theory in Organizations study group, which has allowed me to remain plugged in to this fascinating world. Erik Thompson is one of the leaders of that group and was also my first Bowen coach in Vermont. Kathy Wiseman is another of our leaders, and I learn important things from both of them (and from other members) at every meeting.

Back to the world of family business, I have been a member of the Family Firm Institute (FFI) since 2013 and cannot imagine where I would be without that peer network. I am also a member of a virtual study group through FFI and have begun great professional and personal relationships with a few people there, notably Elle Hansen, Natalie McVeigh and Mairi Mickel, all of whom I was honoured to co-present with.

My truest "tribe," though, is the Purposeful Planning Institute. John A. Warnick is the tireless founder of PPI, and there are few people I look up to more than John A. It is through both PPI and FFI that I managed to meet many other notable people in this area who I am proud to think of as friends as well, including Jim Grubman and Dennis Jaffe. If you liked this book and have not yet read any of theirs, I recommend them all.

Closer to home, my own business coach, Melissa Dawn, has helped guide me in almost everything I do, along with Tarek Riman, who handles my online presence from A to Z. I was lucky enough to start with them before they both became bestselling authors and thank them for all they've helped me to do much better than I could have managed if left to my own devices.

My own family of origin cannot go without mention, from my late father, Stefan, and mother, Magdalena, who raised me right, along with my sisters, Linda and Christine. We continue to have our family meetings, along with Tom Chinappi, the brother I never had and the one I always refer to whenever I try to explain the importance of having someone around the table who has a different last name. Tom began working for my dad in the 1980s and he remains our consigliere today.

Lastly, my nuclear family, who seemed only too happy to see me take off for the cottage on numerous occasions to write this book. My wife, Julie, whom I met at MBA school in 1989, has encouraged me every step of the way since, especially continuing to insist that I write books.

Our son, Richard, and daughter, Sophie, continue to make their parents proud and have been relatively easy to parent, at least so far. We have enjoyed watching them find their own way in the world, and raising them has given me an important lens into the world of family transitions that I could not have imagined if we had not become parents ourselves.

Lastly, thanks to everyone who has read this book and learned something from it, and hopefully tells others about it.

Made in the USA
Lexington, KY
28 June 2019